Walking
with Arthur

Finding God on My Way to New York

D0029900

James O'Donnell

NORTHFIELD PUBLISHING
CHICAGO

Scripture taken from the *Holy Bible, New International Version*®. NIV®. Copyright © 1973, 1978, 1984 by International Bible Society. Used by permission of Zondervan Publishing House. All rights reserved.

ISBN: 1-881273-67-9
EAN/ISBN-13: 978-1-881273-67-7

Library of Congress Cataloging-in-Publication Data

O'Donnell, James, 1948-
    Walking with Arthur : finding God on my way to New York / by James O'Donnell.
        p. cm.
    ISBN 1-881273-67-9
    1. O'Donnell, James, 1948- 2. Christian biography. I. Title.

BR1725.O39A3 2005
277.3'0828'092—dc22

2004021454

1 3 5 7 9 10 8 6 4 2

Printed in the United States of America

Walking

with Arthur

To Arthur,
who turned me toward the path of wisdom,

And for my three boys,
Nick, Andrew, and Jon,
that they would seek wisdom all their lives,
and might find friends
who help them on their way

CONTENTS

ACKNOWLEDGMENTS

Writing a book is a long, lonely, and frustrating task, however fascinating its subject may once have been to its author. It is also an impossible task to finish well without the help of many others working behind the scenes, offering encouragement as well as all manner of practical help and support in shaping the final product.

Walking with Arthur began with a conversation with my literary agent, John Eames, without whose initial help and guidance, I probably would not have found a publisher. Thank you, John.

At Northfield Publishing, some very special people came to believe early on that *Walking with Arthur* might be of help to others, who seek a good friend or wish to be one. May those who seek, find.

I want to thank Mark Tobey, associate publisher, for taking on the book; and Betsey Newenhuyse, editor *extraordinaire,* for tackling mountains of pages, words, memories, and ideas and sculpting them into what I have come to feel is a very pleasing offering. My thanks also to Janis Backing, publicity manager, who never ceases to try to find people and audiences willing to talk with an author; and Jim Vincent, general editor, who had many wonderful suggestions to polish the end product.

Lastly, I thank my Lizzie. For it is she who has lived almost every moment of *Walking with Arthur.* She was at my side, not just in the writing and in helping with insights and direction, but much more in the living of this lifelong, ongoing transformation. Through it all, she has never given up on me.

As wise Solomon wrote:

> *A wife of noble character who can find?*
> *She is worth far more than rubies.*
> *"Many women do noble things,*
> *but you surpass them all."* (Proverbs 31:10, 29)

"In the middle of my life I came to myself
in the midst of a dark wood."
—Dante, *The Divine Comedy*

PROLOGUE:
1984

1984—that year made so famous by George Orwell—forms the hinge of my life.

It was the year my father, against whom I had struggled so hard, died. It was the year my employer rejiggered my compensation—but only after I had hit the pay ball deep, deep into left field and out of the park. It was the year, too, when our oldest son, then age nine, began talking about killing himself. And it was the year I decided to divorce my wife, Lizzie.

It was a year of very big stuff!

Yet 1984 was also the year in which, while trying to cope with or run from these enormous challenges, I found I believed in nothing. I held nothing sacred. I trusted no one. And no one I knew was worth trusting.

That is, until I met Arthur.

It's hard now to recall how I looked at the world in 1984. For no matter how hard I try to remember the details of what was important to me back then, I can't. It's too long ago. What I do remember, though, is that I didn't believe in anyone or anything beyond myself. And because I didn't, money and networks were what I thought were the most important things in the world. In other words, money and networks were gods to me because they could get me the best in life.

As I look back on the person I was in 1984, I don't like him very much.

I think I was lost in myself and in my own self-righteousness, desiring to and believing I could control my life and anybody else's that intersected with mine. Full of surface bravado, I was also, often, full of contempt for those who were different or who crossed me. And full of fear that I might lose or fail.

For years I commuted into New York City from the leafy northern suburb of Pelham, New York. Arriving early in Grand Central Station, I'd fight my way across the dizzying traffic patterns of everyone else in the rail terminal to get to Zaro's Bakery. There, impatient, I might overhear a woman in front of me taking too long, chatting with the clerk about street people she fed daily.

"The whole wheat bagels look good this morning. Why don't you give me a half dozen for my friends on the street?"

People like that irked me. They took my time, and, worse they encouraged "them"—the street people we had too many of. Seemed "stupid" to encourage tax-burdening losers.

In 1984, I thought such thoughts.

"Put them to work," I'd hear myself thinking, in line at Zaro's.

It was my turn. "One bagel. Plain. No, nothing else. That's all. Thank you."

Then, passing by the bums and homeless in corridors and doorways of the terminal, I'd be on my way, out of Grand Central. On the street, invariably, I'd meet more "bums and winos" sleeping off a binge as productive society went off to make money. In the mid-1980s these riffraff seemed to litter the streets of midtown Manhattan like old snow in winter.

Often on my way to the office I'd spot one particular sandwichboard man threatening those passing him by with eternal damnation unless we "repent and believe."

Thank God, I thought, I'd been spared "this religious garbage" growing up. For I considered myself one of the "enlightened"—the modern people, who knew religion was only for fools and failures.

A week later I might find myself traveling for business to Europe, the West Coast or, one time in particular, to Chicago. It was evening, the end of a long, hard day—as all my days were. Few, I thought, worked as hard or as smart as I. I always gave it my all, and now deserved a nice place to stay and a good meal.

That night I happened to be at the Hyatt, near O'Hare airport. It was after eight, and the dining room was empty, except for an attractive woman at a distant table. She was alone too.

"What if . . ." I begin thinking.

"This is OK," I think.

"I'm a good guy," my mind spins into overdrive, "because if I were ever to fall into adultery, it wouldn't be with a hooker, like some of my fancy friends in New York City, nor would I shack up with somebody else's wife looking for a one-night fling. No, that kind of stuff is wrong, beneath me. But if I just happen to stumble into a one-night fling in Chicago, with a nice looking woman . . . now that would be different, wouldn't it?"

Or so I thought back in 1984.

As I say, I don't like the person I was back then.

In meeting Arthur, in 1984, I awoke as if from a long sleep. From a lifetime of self-absorption, I awoke to want to learn about the purpose and meaning of life.

I'm writing this book to encourage men, especially, to seek good friends—not any friends. Men need to look for friends who will help them discover what's important in life. I hope men will talk to each other about the kinds of things my friend Arthur talked to me about.

What did Arthur and I talk about? We talked about the world we live in, our lives, our families, and our work, of course. But we also talked about the culture we swim in every day, a culture particularly unfriendly to people who seek to live meaningful lives. Uncertain of how to talk to each other, we sniffed around like dogs at a fire hydrant before learning how to ask each other hard questions. Once we started asking such questions, we discovered we didn't agree with each other on everything. Still, we tried to be real with each other, even when we didn't know for sure what was real or true. Sometimes, we read a particular book and talked about it. We did a lot of things together. We saw a few movies and ate lunch with each other once in a while. Sometimes, we went for long walks and went on trips together, as we did once when we went skiing with two of my young boys, because Arthur wanted to try to be like a grandfather to them.

For they didn't have one.

What follows, then, are some things that two friends talked about during five special years together. Our conversations appear in no particular order, though they are linked by the common hope that men might learn, grow, discover, and desire the good life—the *really* good life, that is.

This is a story about the great good that real friendship can do. It's a story about my friend Arthur, how we met, what we did, what we talked about, and the profound effect his friendship has had on my life. I hope you have—or one day will have—such a friend, because such a friend is priceless in the confusion and difficulty that life holds for us.

I hope you find a good friend with whom to share your own life and to grow wise, as good and wise a friend as Arthur was to me. May you find that someone, or may you come to *desire* to find such a friend—someone with whom you can share trivia as well as search out the deepest riches of wisdom. I hope you find a friend who not only watches *Monday Night Football* with you but who challenges your deepest convictions.

For me, that someone came into my life in 1984.

WEEKDAY
WARRIORS

My office on the 57th floor of a midtown Manhattan skyscraper may have been lofty, but in the world of business, I still looked up to some whose power or larger offices exceeded mine. Their positions only deepened my commitment to money and networking.

Some pursued power much more than I did. I was more interested in just the money—and in the networks it brought. But is any of this surprising? What better place to put your trust than in money or networks, if you don't know what is more important?

I worked with lots of very smart people who, like myself, had beautiful Ivy League educations. We competed ferociously with each other and knew lots about yachts, designer suits, jumbo mortgages, and discounted cash flows. But our educations hadn't taught us much about real relationships—or maybe we just couldn't remember. At work, I don't remember hearing one thing about philosophical or spiritual things, either, except perhaps for some nuggets that might get a laugh at a party. Yet, here we were, running the world. Or at least making enough money to think we were. Who knew more than we did about real life—the "good life," that is—and how to get it and keep it, than people like us?

Yet, as I look back on those years, when I think about all that would happen to me and to our family a decade later, I'm astonished how little I knew about anything worth knowing. How poor, too, were my instincts—other than in business—about how to learn and grow in a confusing and challenging world. But, then, before I met Arthur, I didn't know anyone else who knew more than I did.

But I do remember overhearing conversations about what was important stuff. They woke me up. They made me pay attention, knowing something important was being said. And though I didn't know any better, I knew somehow that what I was hearing wasn't right. But the people I was overhearing didn't know any more than I did. Maybe money and networks were not the most important things to get through life. But I didn't want to think about that.

A perk of my job gave me membership in a swanky health club on Park Avenue, a few blocks from my 57th floor office in Rockefeller Center, from where I had a beautiful view of Central Park. I worked out at that gym three times a week at lunch time. The place filled up with successful men, and a few women.

One day, while in the locker room, I overheard an older guy—a few years older than me, about forty—kidding a guy in his twenties about getting married. The older guy teased him: "Why pick a flower when you can enjoy the garden?" I knew the older guy only meant to be cute. But as an "older" guy myself—in my mid-thirties —struggling in a troubled marriage, and trying to hold on, cynical wisdom like the older guy's was just another ax blow to the tree that I'd already whacked too often myself. His joke was clever, but, I wondered, is that all marriage is—a cynical joke? Is that all we bright guys from the best schools, with great jobs, can say about marriage? Make jokes about it?

Back then, I didn't know any better. But something in me still wanted to believe there was something more to marriage, whatever it might be. I didn't know what. But I knew that my own view of marriage was as cynical—and hopeless—as the guy making a joke.

Another time, at the same gym, I overheard a sadder conversation, meant to be private. A guy, obviously in pain and feeling embarrassment, was telling one of his buddies he was divorcing. I didn't think they knew I was listening. So I tried to be inconspicuous, by retying my sneakers or adjusting and readjusting my socks. I wanted to know what another bright, successful guy from my world might tell his friend about the trauma he was heading into. Conversations like this were rare in the world I belonged to. We didn't talk about feelings or failure. Those kinds of things were woman stuff. They weren't shared among us heavy hitters, for we knew that appearances were reality. Seeming to be out of control was as good as being out of control. We avoided letting others know a lot about us, for knowledge could be used against us. Being guarded—with charm—was best.

Even though I knew it wasn't right to listen in, I ached for some wisdom on divorce. But as was almost always the case back then, my listening was worthless. The older guy said nothing to his hurting buddy, except that "it was probably for the best." And that, "Hey, we learn from such things."

Could he be right? I wondered.

Then another time, on a Friday, I found myself at an important business meeting away from my office. I had arrived a little early. Sitting at an elegant conference table, waiting with my muffin and orange juice for the start of the meeting, I sat close to the senior executive who was going to run the meeting, the guy who had asked me to say a few words to his staff. Directly across from me and to the left of the senior executive was his director of human resources.

I had just sat down when the senior exec and his human resource guy got caught up in a very audible conversation. A sensitive one, too, I thought. It was about an executive the senior guy wanted fired. Given the guy's level, however, the HR guy suggested it best be done on a Monday, or so research said, the HR guy claimed.

"On a Monday? Why, Phil?" the senior executive demanded.

"Well, it gives the poor guy the rest of the week to absorb the shock. He can tell his family when he's ready. Saves some dignity. He might even keep leaving for work for a few days without his family's knowing he'd been fired."

Bruce, the senior guy, was unimpressed. "So what am I supposed to do? Wait to tell him and ruin *my* weekend?"

Now, neither Bruce nor the two guys giving advice in the locker room were, that I know, philosophers or therapists. However, they were successful men, admired and highly respected by their peers as good business people. And in their own ways, they were just trying to respond to unexpected, personal, and potentially difficult, emotional situations. Still, even though I didn't waste my own time thinking about anybody but myself, what I'd overheard in all three conversations struck me, even then, as selfish, self-protective, stupidity. Mind you, at that point, I didn't have anything better to offer, had I been the go-to guy. But some instinct within me was, even then, bubbling up and whispering to me, "Not this."

I am still processing other memories from that time, other stories of very successful people I knew who had little feeling for others or for wanting balance in their lives.

In New York, I had an acquaintance, a top executive, whose first wife had divorced him and taken the kids. Now married again, this time around he wasn't going to miss his new kids' growing up. So every Friday, after school, he sent his limo over to pick up his son, a ten-year-old. The kid had time with his father, but only by coming to Dad's office to watch him work into the night.

There was another guy I knew out West—a top dog, too—who did just fine on four hours of sleep. And because he did, he expected his "direct reports," as he called them, to do the same. But to prove his underlings' mettle and loyalty, the guy held staff meetings late at night or very early in the morning—simply because, as the boss, he could. And he wanted to see how devoted his peons were.

Another guy was so driven to cultivate his kids' minds, both of whom were under ten, that he read *Moby Dick* to them—every day!

At breakfast! Each morning, for months, chapter by chapter, whether the kids wanted to listen or not, he sat them down at the breakfast table and slogged through the book. Then the kids were off to school, and he headed into New York City, where he would lawyer away deep into the night, inspired by what a great father he was.

None of this was the least bit odd to me back then. It was just the way life was, whether you were going someplace or you had already arrived. Successful people had their prerogatives, as well as their quirks; and kids, spouses, or employees had better adjust to them or learn to put up with them—or else! Because the star was not about to change. ("Are you crazy? Why would I?") In fact, you had better change, if you knew what was good for you.

After all, we were the warriors who left our families in the lovely suburbs and rode into battle each day. We were the winners. We were the ones who'd made it in life—not our spouse, nor the kids, nor our underlings. ("What rights or privileges do others have?") We were the successes. We were the ones entitled to the fruits of our accomplishments. Others weren't. At best, others lived off us or received a share of the dividends from our reflected glory, *if* they behaved.

After all, at work, we were catered to. A staff member did our bidding, fetched our left-behinds, and carried coffee for us. ("And you'd better do it quickly too.") If we weren't always clear, then listen up. ("Get used to 'Jimspeak' . . . What's wrong with you?") Yet, at home, we weren't always revered as we were at work. Lizzie even talked back to me and increasingly went her own way. I resented being unappreciated after all I afforded her and the kids.

Back then, I think I was simply a jerk who didn't know it at the time.

IN SEARCH
OF THE
PERFECT HOME

Before you meet Arthur, it may be useful to describe a bit more the person he would befriend; me, in other words. And the person I was, best I can remember. For each of us is part of everything that forms us. Each of us is sort of a living history.

As I look back over my early life, I'm embarrassed by some of what I remember. I'm a lucky duck to have gotten as far as I did. For while some, for sure, endured harsher upbringings, mine was challenging enough. It could have led me into very destructive stuff, had luck—or maybe something called "grace," of which I knew nothing —not intervened.

I grew up in a broken and very unhappy home, not unlike many homes nowadays but less so some fifty years ago. My family carried a lot of pain, and memories of that pain still haunt me.

I was a smart, sensitive kid who grew up searching for what might change the life I knew as a youngster. I lived with my sister and mother in a one-bedroom apartment in the Bronx, where we were frequently visited by my father, who, oddly, chose to live with his mother. Why? I don't know for sure, even today. Of course, as a child, I thought his arrangement was normal.

But my father's choice of bedrooms compounded my mother's tendencies toward anxiety and depression that left her devastated, severely affecting life in our home. Life in the Bronx was a small-scale Fort Apache, a life of fighting and grim silences, followed by tortuous logic and the settling of old scores.

Perhaps my deepest memory of the Bronx was a Halloween when I was about eight. I went to school that day dreaming of the candy I would collect in our apartment building. I wasn't allowed to leave the building that night, but there were six floors with ten apartments on each floor, and enough people in the apartments to cop a stash of candy that could keep me in chocolate dots and kisses for weeks. All day at school I fantasized about the ways I might count my haul, sort it, and organize it on the patterned carpet on our living room floor.

By the time I got home from school, I could barely contain myself. But I couldn't go out until after supper, still a couple of hours away.

I had business to do with the building's superintendent—the "super," as I called him—getting a big pail for apple dunking after I got back from trick-or-treating. The super was a gruff German, but a nice man to me. I wanted the pail so my sister and I could bob for apples. Somebody at school told me it was fun, and I wanted to try it once I got back from ringing bells and yelling "trick or treat" down the halls of 707 E. 241st Street in the Bronx, New York.

I had a hard time sitting at the dinner table that night. I was so excited with my plans for candy and bobbing that eating dinner was a poor distraction. By some time around 8:00, I was done with the trick-or-treating part of my work and couldn't wait for Part 2, my first experience with apple bobbing.

As I approached the door of apartment 4H, where I lived, I could hear my mother screaming at my sister, not a rare event, but this time the yelling was especially loud, even with the door closed. After I rang our bell to be let in, I saw my sister in tears; my mother was furious and red-faced. And then Mom turned on me as well and yelled at us both: "I'm taking both of you to the orphanage. Tomorrow! I don't need toys."

I remember the hot tears welling up in my eight-year-old eyes. My great night of fun was over. The dream of counting and sorting candy amid the patterns of the carpet and dunking for apples crashed and burned in front of me. I stared at the pail I had set out before I'd made my rounds, sitting on the piece of plastic I'd carefully laid out on the living room rug so mom wouldn't get mad at me if we spilled water amid our fun that never happened. Then I tried not to look further at that pail in the middle of the living room, winking at me, mocking me for being such a fool.

After all my preparation and daydreaming, there would be no apple dunking tonight. That year, I never sorted my candy. I'm not sure if, as a child, I ever went out at Halloween again. Years later, as an adult, no Halloween with my own kids would pass without raising painful memories of that night.

That was one of the worst nights of my life. But it was not unique.

Many other times after that night my mother told my sister and me that we were going to the orphanage. We got our share of smacks, too. But the orphanage threats hurt most. Oh, we were slapped around for looking in places we were not supposed to look, or for asking questions that were not supposed to be asked. But none of those left the lasting wound that the orphanage threats did.

My mother's lifelong tendency toward depression and mental illness, and her sense of abandonment by her husband—my father—helps me now understand why she acted as she did. Part of it might also have been a consequence of a wild youth when she married and divorced very young—and had a back-alley abortion—none of which, to her dying day, did she think my sister or I knew about. Ours was a house of secrets, of skeletons too numerous to keep in the few closets we had. But any of which, if my sister or I ever got too close to—say by opening a shoe box under a bed or asking mom why this old bank book had a different name in it—might get us a swift smack in the face.

In the summers, and many days after school, I'd see Dad. He was a "self-made" small businessman, whose own father had died, tragically, when he was only two (as was also the case with my mother). My paternal grandfather was an Irish immigrant who'd worked as a stableman for some fancy people in the Berkshires of western Massachusetts. One November night, in the early part of the last century, Grandpa was, apparently, moving his employer's horses from the summer house to New York City in time for a horse show at Madison Square Garden. The best I can surmise, the horses on a train with him got spooked and started to act up. He was probably trying to calm them when one must have kicked him with such force that he was thrown out of the moving train, probably hit his head, and then slipped under the ice that had already formed on the Housatonic River. A few days later, his body was found at a dam.

My grandfather's death left a widow and three little boys under six (including my future father) with no means of support. So Grandma took jobs such as a "latrine matron" and a housekeeper in New York City to make ends meet before the coming of public assistance. An elderly, unmarried aunt came down from New Haven, Connecticut, to live with the boys while Grandma worked long hours.

Clearly my father, like my mother, had a tough start in life. He grew up to be a cynic, as I became for many years. My dad doubted that anyone, underneath pretending, actually loved anyone. I think he felt people only used each other. I remember early in my marriage visiting him with some new, young, married friends Lizzie and I had made. The Saturday morning my father first laid eyes on our friends, they were on a porch, holding hands, with their backs to him. He came up behind them and said, "Watch that! In a few years, you'll be throwing punches at each other." A typical greeting by a man who craved to be the center of attention and often was, no matter how crude his means to get there.

31

My dad and I fought often about his rudeness to visitors, toll collectors, and waitresses in restaurants, whom he'd humiliate mercilessly if they spoke too fast or didn't say hello quickly enough. He was a real Archie Bunker, if you know the type.

Still, I know he loved me and cared about me. But in my mid-twenties, when he came to a meeting of a community organization I'd become involved in and stood up in the middle of a speaker's presentation to berate him, I hit the roof. And he called Lizzie "clammo," for whatever reason, after I'd fallen in love with her.

Yikes! Did we ever fight over that one—big time!

But while I rejected much of my father's attitudes and prejudices, I unconsciously adopted some of his pushy, aggressive style. Like him, I could become forceful, determined, even mean, if people crossed me.

Having seen the destructive consequences of my parents' marriage, I grew up thinking that, one day, I would create a perfect marriage, a wonderful, loving family, and a magnificently fulfilling career. But for reasons I still don't understand, I also grew up searching for what life might mean beyond those prizes, all of which were in my power to create.

I had not, of course, grown up in what I might call today, a "spiritual" home. But somehow, maybe because of the unhappiness I'd known, I wondered what life was all about. What are we all doing here? I don't think I was particularly precocious, intellectually speaking. I didn't come to any great "Aha's!" But those moments of youthful curiosity led, more than once, to speculations about God. I wondered, for instance, if God existed. And if he or she or it existed, what was God like? Might God be a cosmic cop, walking around the parapets of heaven, with a clipboard, and thunderbolts, taking names and throwing fits, like my mother? Or, might God be like the gentler Jesus I learned about in Catholic school (except when the nuns smacked my knuckles with a ruler)?

Frankly, I never came to any sure opinion, and I don't think my understanding of spiritual things ever got much beyond a fourth grader's level.

As the years passed, religion interested me less and less, while I grew more serious about earthly things, especially career and family. And my autonomy. And making money.

I grew increasingly interested in doing well in this world. Thinking I was only being realistic, I believed life would give me only what I earned, taking the breaks as they came. Anything else was, at best, highly speculative. In other words, faith in anything beyond me was unknown when things went well (because I'd made those moments); and faith was merely clutching and desperate when things went poorly. But at such moments, I wasn't above grabbing any help I could get.

How different my friends in high school seemed. They all wanted freedom *from* homes which, unintentionally, smothered their natural instincts for freedom. While I, on the other hand, craved finding or making a home where I would be more than just a "boarder." The home I would create would be perfect. It would be filled with love and harmony.

In the summer of 1967, I fell in love with Lizzie, the girl I had met backstage when I was in a play in upstate New York. By day, I taught tennis; at night, I acted in community theater. Teaching tennis helped pay for college. After we married in 1971, I envisioned creating that perfect home for my Lizzie and our exceptional (yet-to-be- born) kids who would never grieve their parents nor be exposed to parents fighting or having long, silly disagreements about television shows or politics, as I had been growing up. No, in our home there would only be, as the Beatles sang it back then, "love, love, love"—just ecstasies of intimacy and tenderness.

At least, that was my fantasy.

What Lizzie and I got, instead, by the time I met Arthur, were two bright, handsome boys, the older of whom wrestled so seriously with depression that our entire family had been in therapy from the time he was six. By age twelve, in 1987, in spite of the best help we could get, he wanted to kill himself, and twice, halfheartedly, tried to. As a consequence of the unhappiness of this precious young boy, a deep sense of failure crept into our lives as parents.

Both Lizzie and I felt, in the midst of our outwardly pretty lives, powerless, ashamed, and heartsick. No matter how hard we tried, we seemed to be incompetent parents. Yet it was not to each other that we turned in our sadness. Rather, we grew suspicious of the part the other played in why this had happened. We grew unsure of each other's abilities or willingness to do right about the future. Could we, as a couple, handle the next crisis, whatever it might be?

Then, too, there was my work.

When Lizzie and I married, I was a high school English teacher, making $7,100 a year, and content with that. We were both happy. Partly because, by the mid-1970s, we had moved to a place we had dreamed of living since we'd met in 1967. It was where the theater was, where we'd met. In 1974, I found a teaching job in this idyllic mountaintop setting in upstate New York. From the porch of the crumbling house Lizzie and I began to fix up, we had a seventy-mile view. What more could one ask for?

However, for me, the bloom was soon off the rose. Somehow, it just wasn't perfect enough. While I was not miserable, I somehow thought I could be, or should be, wildly happy. From where this inability to experience contentment came, I don't know. But that's the way I was, often: less than thrilled by the best life offered me. Somehow always thinking, "Is this all there is?"

I always wanted more. Lots more! Not necessarily more money or power or possessions, but I wanted to be wildly happy, and somehow, immaturely, I expected I could be—all the time! Especially after the childhood I'd endured. I felt owed happiness by this world and everyone in it.

So, for no better reason than that the grass must be greener in graduate school, I left my teaching job in the idyllic place Lizzie loved, not even asking for her opinion, and went off to Columbia University, in New York City, to get an MBA. Why an MBA? Because in the summers, in our lovely little mountaintop community a lot of investment bankers came up to vacation with their families, and from a number of casual conversations with them, I thought they held the keys to the good life—which was money! Soon, I too began to think that making more money was the way to joy. And, soon, I was out to make my fortune.

While I was a very good student, business school didn't thrill me, either. Oh, I did well enough. But I still didn't know what I wanted to do in my life. Despite pursuing an MBA, I wasn't sure I still wanted to go into business. Something important was still missing. The smart people at school—the ones I admired—were going after the high-paying investment banking jobs. That confirmed where I should head too. After all, I had all those friends back on the mountaintop from the summer rooting for me to go into investment banking.

But when I graduated from Columbia, I didn't get a single job offer from an investment bank, and so, with a new knot of sadness and failure to untie, I was led to explore other things.

I became a certified public accountant. Yet in spite of luxurious European business travel, being a CPA and having an MBA didn't wind my watch any more than had living in a mountaintop paradise.

But being a CPA led me into the money management business, a kind of poor cousin to the sex and glamour of investment banking. There, by 1984, I was making hundreds of thousands of dollars a year. Yet the more money I made, the more unhappy I seemed to become. I was convinced my employer was robbing me blind, and I threatened to sue him to recover my stolen money—my hardearned money. Still clueless as to what mattered in life, money now seemed no more satisfying to me than teaching had.

Even more regrettably, my life with Lizzie had been bruised by my obsessions and inconsideration. By 1984, she began moving off into her own separate endeavors in which she might find herself more appreciated.

And so there I was, a thirty-five-year-old guy with more money than I had ever dreamed I'd make, with a wife who could barely stand to be in the same room with me, and with at least one child struggling merely to survive.

If people looked at me, they might, on the outside, not have imagined a luckier, smarter, more successful, "well-put-together" guy. But on the inside, something was terribly wrong.

Right about this time, at the church Lizzie and I attended once in a while—to give our two boys a good moral grounding—we had a new minister. And though I had long since drifted away from attending church regularly or feeling any conviction about the intrinsic value of joining one, I did follow, from a safe distance, the congregation's selection of a new minister. Once he arrived, I felt strangely drawn to seek a nighttime chat with him. Why? I really don't know. Probably out of nothing more than ego and pride. I wanted this guy to know who I was and to know how the church had failed me and our family. After all, in my warped economy, the church *owed* me, like everyone and everything else did.

But perhaps, even at this early moment in my awakening, I was reaching out for something more significant than what I'd chased after so far. More significant, that is, than making more money. Or endlessly trying to satisfy *me*. For even now, I think, under all my brashness and bravado I was someone who desperately wanted something to fill up my unfathomable emptiness.

Who knows? Just maybe this was a strange, first longing to know God; but if not God, then certainly something or someone beyond myself. Whatever it was, it was still going to be on my own terms. In other words, I don't think I was seeking dramatic change. After all, to me, I didn't need change.

No, it was all those terrible, inconsiderate people who polluted my glittering but unappreciated life who needed to change. Besides, there wasn't anything big wrong with *me*. It was obvious everyone else was screwed up and, because of that, they were giving me a hard time. I was basically fine. Oh, maybe I could use some smoothing out of some small, rough spots. And, of course, I could always use more understanding from others. But smoothed out or not, understood or not, I was one neat guy. No changes were really needed in me, thank you very much.

Well, you might imagine my surprise—and my horror—when Don, the new minister, whom I had just berated in my "welcome-to-our-church" speech, responded to my crankiness by inviting me to join a men's spiritual growth group, which he was, just then, in the process of forming.

"What do you think, Jim? Can I count on you to come?"

I was speechless.

Imagine! A men's spiritual growth group! A prayer circle, or something like that. "Whoa!" I thought, "Is this guy clueless or what! Like telling one of my buddies in New York that sucking lollipops would increase investment performance. What do you say to such a clown?"

Oh, the fun I had imagining the weirdos and losers who would show up for something like that!

But how little I knew.

For it would be at that very meeting of supposed "weirdos and losers" that I would come to know Arthur, who would have such a profound impact on my sorry life.

MEETING
ARTHUR

The death of my dad. The suicidal thoughts of my oldest son. My own thoughts of divorcing Lizzie. The events that befell me in 1984 softened me up and prepared me to meet Arthur. At that time, he was in his late fifties, about twenty years older than I, and a lawyer on Wall Street. We both had two degrees from Ivy League schools, but his came from Harvard—in nuclear physics and law, no less. That's what first got my attention. His credentials gave him instant credibility. I believed in that old saying: "You can always tell a Harvard man, but you can't tell him much."

While it was the small group at church where I truly got to know Arthur, my earliest memory of him goes back to one autumn weekend afternoon. I was out mowing my grass or pulling weeds or doing some Saturday afternoon chore. Arthur walked by with his dog. He stopped and introduced himself. We talked for a few minutes. I remember him smiling. He seemed confident, a comfortable man meeting a stranger—a good sign, to me, a sign of authority and ability. I respected such signs.

Apparently, Arthur, along with his wife, had just moved into our lovely neighborhood from another leafy New York suburb, farther up the Long Island shoreline. He'd moved in to tend to his elderly, widowed father. He'd actually grown up in the house he moved back into.

I had no adult male friends in the fall of 1984. I wasn't looking for any, either. But as things worked out, on many a morning I found myself running into Arthur during the few minutes it took me to get to the Pelham train station. Sometimes, we walked together, never by plan but, I guess, simply because we happened to be on the same schedule.

It took only about seven minutes to walk from my front door to the station; a little longer from Arthur's house. If we met along the way, we'd share a few words. Once on the train, at first, we might or might not sit together. Later on, I came to hope we'd run into each other, giving me a chance to sit with him on the half-hour ride to Grand Central Station. As I got to know him, I liked him more and more, and began to learn much that I'd soon treasure.

In the course of our unplanned walks to the station—sometimes, more like a dash—and the trips into New York City, Arthur asked me important questions and shared his own life. As I look back, I think he must have chosen the words he shared with me with the utmost care. Like the lawyer he was, he'd share a bit about himself and then ask me about my own life, always listening for my motivations. I can't remember a time when I ever felt threatened by his questions.

His manner was always gentle. Besides, his way was always to share first, and usually more than he expected of me or, certainly, more than I expected a man to share. Also, when we talked, he looked at me deeply, and he listened. He spoke carefully too. And, maybe most surprisingly, he remembered.

One time, I told him our younger son was home from school for a day or two. He had a cold or flu, or something kids get. Several days later, when I again ran into Arthur on the walk to the train, he asked me how Andrew was doing. For a moment, I couldn't remember what he was asking about. By then, I'd forgotten little Andrew had been sick. But Arthur hadn't forgotten, and suddenly, I remembered: I had shared news of Andrew's illness with Arthur. His remembering that kind of detail impressed me. It was unlike me or any other guy I knew. Guys I knew just didn't remember such stuff, even about our own kids.

That same fall, once in a while, we also began to meet for lunch in New York City. Arthur was getting to know me, and I him. As time went on, he was also sharing himself with me with what seemed like an almost uncomfortable level of vulnerability. But Arthur did it naturally. He wasn't morbidly self-critical, nor was he an emotional exhibitionist. No, he was simply honest and appropriate in what he shared. Even helpful.

I was taken aback, because I'd never met a man before who shared important, personal details of his life to help a younger friend. I began to wonder, nice as this guy was, "What is his 'angle'?" To me, everybody had an angle, because information was power. Vulnerability was weakness. Or stupidity. Whatever it was, it gave the "other guy" the upper hand. But Arthur wasn't stupid. Yet, here he was, a Wall Street lawyer, with two degrees from Harvard, at some of the nicest eating spots in New York, telling me about his life.

Even his divorce.

Yes, his divorce. And I wanted to know about his divorce. I wanted to know everything! Because I was on the edge of divorcing Lizzie. And given the cheap wisdom I trafficked in inside an elegant locker room in midtown Manhattan, and based on the investment logic I championed to handle life's problems, I surely wanted to know what Arthur thought about divorce.

Turned out, he didn't like it. But I wanted to know more.

Arthur told me that, years before, his first wife wanted a divorce. He said she thought it would be best for them and their five kids. She thought Arthur didn't love her, that he didn't talk enough, that he was a distant father. It was the same sort of stuff I might have said about Lizzie. When Arthur's first wife told him she wanted a divorce, Arthur recalled he thought it would be a mistake, but, somehow, he didn't fight it. So he and his wife got divorced. Simple as that. Seemed back then, Arthur didn't much believe in anything either.

Then almost as a throwaway, he said, "It would be several years before I met Jesus—"

Whoa! "Met Jesus"!? Did I hear that right? Is Arthur kidding? I wondered, feeling my palms getting sweaty. I began blinking uncontrollably, squirming a bit, but acted, I'm sure, as if a waiter just owed me my soup.

Arthur went on to say that he looked back on his divorce as one of the great mistakes of his life, in spite of the wonderful woman he had later married. He said his kids' lives hadn't been improved either. Nor his wife's. Nor his own for many years.

"But I didn't know that then," he confessed, sadly.

"Know what?" I asked. "What was there to know?"

"That, in most cases, divorce is wrong. But because it's quick, and often, very easy, it might seem to be right. That it hurts people. That the promise of lives bettered by splitting up is a lie most of the time.

"That's what I didn't know.

"Yet, my wife and I went to church for years. At church I was even an elder. I was a nice guy, a good person. And yet I believed in nothing. Nothing was important enough to get worked up over, to believe in passionately."

I sat there, speechless for a moment. Arthur was the first guy I'd met who talked like this, who seemed to talk about things other than pro sports or where to get good ribs. And for starters today, he was talking about divorce.

Arthur's honesty made a space in my own life, into which I began to feel I could share a little bit about myself and my own struggles. We both knew we were fortunate people to live as we did, and where we did. And we both knew there were almost as many broken homes in our neighborhood as there were manicured lawns. So I 'fessed up to Arthur that I was thinking of divorcing Lizzie.

He asked, "Why?"

I said I didn't know. But his question made me think.

After a long pause, I added, "A lot of reasons, I guess. Some big, some small. We just don't get along with each other any more."

I couldn't yet bring myself to tell Arthur that what I really wanted was someone who would get naked with me and swing from a chandelier as we made love. As if that might make me wildly happy.

But Lizzie wasn't much into swinging from chandeliers, naked or otherwise.

Arthur looked deeply into me and was quiet for a while, but didn't judge me. He listened and asked good questions with tenderness and sincerity. In the end, he said, "Jim, I hope you and Lizzie will try to get some good help and counseling."

And then he delivered the clincher: "And I'll pray for you."

There it was again—like slamming a fist on a table full of soup bowls and watching the soup fly all over the linen. That's how the prayer comment—and the Jesus comment—sounded to me. They were embarrassing.

Yet Arthur wasn't one of those little, old Italian ladies I saw on the streets of New York, dressed in black and reciting the rosary. He wasn't one of those poor souls standing on the street corner, the sandwich-board guys, handing out leaflets about going to hell. But he was speaking in that same code.

"Jesus," he'd said. And then, "I'll pray for you."

Nobody I knew said those things seriously. I didn't know what to say. I felt embarrassed. For him.

But for me too.

I wanted to say, "Are you serious, Arthur? Get hold of yourself with this Jesus nonsense." But somehow, without asking, I knew he was serious. He was too sincere not to be. Too genuine. Too honest.

But I still wondered, "Does he really believe there is someone out there to pray to? And how would he know? What would that someone, or something, out there—that he or she or it—say back?"

Questions like that flooded me. But I didn't ask them that day. I wouldn't have known how to. I needed more time. Up until that moment, I'd never thought about this kind of stuff as an adult. Back in a literature class in college where we read the Bible as myth and talked about God as a symbol, yes, back then, we talked a little about such things. Or said *God* in a curse, perhaps. But I'd dismissed stuff like this long ago as being juvenile—like believing in Santa Claus or the Easter Bunny.

But here was Arthur, the Harvard-educated lawyer, no kid and no dope. He believed this stuff! These irrelevant religious issues—irrelevant, I thought, at least to those who went to the schools Arthur and I had gone to, or lived in places we did. Or worked in jobs like ours.

When Arthur mentioned "Jesus" and told me he would "pray for me," it was as if he'd just said he'd pooped in his pants: It was simply not what polite people I knew talked about. Yet, there he was, hoisting up his faith like dirty underwear on a flagpole for all to see.

Arthur said "Jesus," and he wasn't even cursing!

But no sooner had I heard evidence of Arthur's faith than I began to think about my own. Maybe it was his Harvard degrees again working on my jealous imagination, but I began to wonder: "If a bus ran over me on Madison Avenue, and the morgue called Lizzie to fill out my death certificate, what box on the form would she tell them to check for my religion?"

In my mind, I pictured Lizzie, in grief and confusion, puzzled by the question, "Was he a Jew, a Christian, a Buddhist, a Hindu, an atheist, or what?"

And I imagined Lizzie saying, "Why, he was a Christian. At least, I think he was."

After all, to us, lots of polite people were Christians, weren't they? Wasn't that what made them Christians? Politeness? And wasn't I polite too? At least in public, whenever I wanted to impress someone? In those situations I could be a matchless gentleman.

But Arthur was much more than a gentleman. Much more than a churchgoer, too, or a sectarian believer. He turned out to be the first person I ever met who actually thought about his beliefs *and* his behavior. And it was he who, in time, would challenge my own beliefs and assumptions about what maturity and commitment meant. And because he had a good mind and wanted to grow, he asked me questions that I will wrestle with for the rest of my life. Questions about my faith, of course, but more surprisingly, questions about my work, my family, the world we live in, and my responsibilities to those both near and far.

By December of 1984, a couple of months after the new minister had invited me to the men's group at his church, I was still laughing about who might go to such a thing. His invitation seemed to be such a joke.

"What does a minister know about life?" I wondered. "These guys are paid to play nice." But by December, just a couple of months after I'd met Arthur on my front lawn, everything was different. Because now Arthur asked me if I wanted to go to that same small group. By then, I'd gotten to know him. By then, we'd walked to the train a couple of dozen times, eaten lunch together in NYC, talked and shared more with each other than I'd ever done with anybody before, and I'd learned Arthur was a "player"—with his two degrees from Harvard and his Wall Street law practice.

But now it was time to go beyond playing. It was time for me to start thinking about things far deeper than Wall Street weekday warriors usually wrestle with.

MEETING
ARTHUR'S FRIENDS
. . . AND GOD

"This guy must know a thing or two about life," I began to think.

Arthur the lawyer and Harvard grad was interested in deeper things than making a buck and buying the latest BMW. That's why I accepted the invitation from Arthur and the pastor to meet at Arthur's church at 7:00 a.m. on Sunday mornings. Yes, seven o'clock on a Sunday morning.

I planned to go just once, for Arthur's sake, to show him what a good guy I was. A real friend, who understood the symmetry of friendship.

I thought my going to this "thing"—his thing—would make him happy. He'd feel supported, whatever this stupidity was all about, maybe like a political fund-raiser. For I understood those things.

So the one time I planned to go happened to be in late December 1984. I was nervous. But I'd known Arthur for about three months, and he'd done nothing to make me think my faith in him was misguided. He told me that I might find the prayer group "interesting"—whatever that might mean. I found it hard to believe. Still, I went: to be a good friend to Arthur.

But just to be safe, I took my checkbook along, thinking maybe —just maybe—all along Arthur only wanted a donation to some cause but was too polite to ask me.

I should have known better, however, even that early in our friendship.

Back then, though, I trusted nobody. In fact, by going to Arthur's group, I thought I might be stepping into the world of the truly loony—you know, where I'd find the ones who talk in tongues or who tell jokes using Scripture, like some New York tax lawyers do using the Internal Revenue Code. I felt, quite possibly, I was going to be humiliated when asked my favorite Bible verse or hymn. Or, maybe—God forbid!—to pray out loud.

But nothing like that happened.

For, as I had already found with Arthur, I was being introduced to the courtesy of eternal love. After Arthur introduced me, the men greeted me warmly as Arthur's friend. Then these six men, gathered in a chilly room in late December, let me be a fly on the wall. They went about sharing a little of their personal lives as friends and offered concern for each other. That part lasted about forty-five minutes. Then they prayed out loud for the health of each other and their families, and that their work would glorify God. They also prayed that they would face life's challenges with courage, and finally, they closed with prayers for the needs of the larger world. One even included me in his simple prayer, thanking God that I had joined them that morning, and hoping that my life might be blessed.

Then it was over. Like a warm bath, but one the likes of which I'd never experienced before.

Arthur walked me out.

As was his custom, he thanked me for coming with him and, without any pleading, invited me to come again, if I wanted to. He'd be glad to take me.

Always, that was Arthur's way: never insisting, never embarrassing me by pointing out what I didn't know or hadn't done.

I don't think I said a word to Arthur after the meeting, because I didn't know what to say. I didn't have a vocabulary to process what I had just witnessed. Arthur may have felt my silence after that meeting as disappointment. But I wasn't. It was more inner turmoil. Going in, I expected nothing. I was hoping only to get out alive, yet thinking nothing could happen that I couldn't control. But when I came out I was deeply moved, even if confused. I didn't think a prayer group could touch me, but it did. The men's honesty and concern for each other—and for me—moved me, not any theology that may have been underneath. How simple and direct these men were, as if they believed, sincerely, that they were praying to someone, whoever that might be.

So I went back a second time. And, then, a third time. Ultimately, I joined this little group. For, in that little gathering of men that Arthur introduced me to, I found something I'd been looking for all my life. Something my cynicism had come to disbelieve might even exist. Something precious, meaningful, innocent, and unashamed. Something that hinted of a Someone beyond time or space, a Someone who, before, I would have laughed at, but now I wondered about for the first time.

And then, not so slowly, my skeptical, intellectual, elitist shell that disbelieved in what I could not see or hold began to fall away. So did my belief that we lived in an uncaring world in which we were going to get hurt unless we stood our ground and defended ourselves. That, too, began to peel away, layer by layer, like the skins of an onion.

By February 1985, I'd known Arthur six months. At first, I'd been flabbergasted that a Wall Street lawyer from Harvard believed in fairy tales. Never full of himself, or quick to give pat answers when asked about his faith, Arthur smiled like a bashful boy.

Often he told me that he hadn't expected coming to faith, either. Long after his divorce, maybe in a moment of weakness, he'd agreed to go on a retreat. And it was that retreat that wound up changing his life. Now he suggested I go on the same thing. I might like it, he thought. I might find it meaningful.

This was vintage Arthur: never insisting on anything. But it was those gentle suggestions that, ultimately, transformed my life.

That same February, Arthur sponsored me for one of those retreats he'd gone on. *Tres Dias* it was called—or "three days." Our weekend was scheduled for April. Privately, I was scared about what I was getting into, but I was beginning to trust another human being, and that felt good. Arthur hadn't failed me yet.

Now, at about this same time, perhaps March, Arthur invited me to a dinner party at his home. He wanted me to meet a few friends. I think he wanted me to experience the company of other people of faith, but I dreaded going. Still, for Arthur, I went.

In spite of knowing him for about six months by then, and having attended his Sunday morning group for about three months, I was still afraid that, this time—or some time—I was, at last, going to meet the zanies I knew were out there. Or maybe "Holy Rollers"! Or narrow-minded bigots. Or holier-than-thou prigs, who would press me to confess what I really, really, really thought about St. Gounelibah or the Third Book of Hezekiah, or some other nonsense. Things I knew nothing about, and cared even less to discover. In going to Arthur's party, I had to focus on going just because I was Arthur's friend. Because he'd suggested this. And I knew he was having an incredible influence on my life.

Arthur may also have tried to convince me that meeting his friends would help me understand the kind of people I'd likely meet on my upcoming weekend. He thought I'd be more comfortable if I sensed I had something in common with them. Sounded screwy to me; I felt I was still in for mortal embarrassment.

Though Arthur's instincts had been flawless, this time I expected a bomb. Arthur even used a new word on me: "fellowship." Sounded weird, like people smoking dope. "Fellowship" was not a comforting term. Frankly, it scared me. Sounded pious, sanctimonious . . . phony, too.

But I ended up going to Arthur's party. And though I was, at first, probably a most awkward guest, my first taste of fellowship—whatever the term meant—turned out to be another little bit of heaven, like Sunday morning had become. That surprised me. Again, Arthur was right.

His friends at the dinner party radiated the same kind of real-world faith, hope, and love that I'd come to find in Arthur and in our Sunday morning group. It was like light passing through an ice sculpture, warming me and everything in its path. But it took me time to allow the light in.

At the dinner table, I overheard a strange conversation from a woman sitting next to me, who was talking to the person beyond her. They were both laughing, and I heard an expression I'd never heard before, something like "slain in the Spirit." And as soon as my neighbor turned my way she caught my surprise. Maybe, too, ahead of time, Arthur had warned her there'd be a "newbie" in the room. Once she saw my face, my dinner neighbor turned back to me, still smiling, a little startled, and said very gently that she was sorry.

Of course, I told her there was no need to apologize. But she thought she might have been talking too loud or might have said something I didn't understand or found strange. There was no need, she said. Then, she began to talk to me, very friendly, never asking me a single question that could cause embarrassment. She asked about my family and what I liked to do in my spare time. She turned out to be a sort of female version of Arthur, I guess. I never saw her again.

Every one of Arthur's friends was just as kind. Still, I kept wondering: "What's their angle?" They had to have one. So, in spite of their kindness, I pretty much kept my mouth shut.

Through his friendship with me, Arthur showed me the God I didn't yet believe in. He showed me Jesus too, perhaps, in the only way I would then have been able to understand Him—through friendship with a gracious human being. For years, Arthur befriended, mentored, and instilled hope in me. But I was not the only object of his bounty. He blessed many others, too.

He started a soup kitchen, for instance, in a poor urban area just north of New York City. More than once, as he approached retirement, he went over to meet with a city councilman in Mount Vernon, New York. Arthur offered the city his legal services for free. But the councilman, who also directed an agency formed by a group of churches to assist the poor, told him that Mount Vernon needed food and clothing more than they needed an Ivy League lawyer. But in Arthur, they got both.

As I watched and learned from Arthur, I saw a new model of an adult man, so different from my cronies at work. I saw a Christian man seeking to live out a purposeful existence, serving his God and helping others. In him, I saw a man trying to do right and always willing to think through what "doing right" might be.

From the very beginning, I asked Arthur my hardest questions, the kind of questions that I thought made faith impossible to accept. Like, how did he know God existed, or that Jesus was real? Or, how did he know Jesus was the one true God, and what did that mean? Or, with so much suffering in the world, how could he be-lieve God is loving or powerful?

"How do you know, Arthur, given the mess the world is in, that God answers prayer? Or is even there to hear it? Why do the good suffer as much as those who don't give a rip?"

Arthur never recoiled from my nagging questions, nor did he seem to have a compulsive need to explain the ways of God. I learned as much from his silences and his manners as from his words. He didn't become defensive or irritable. He didn't defend God against all the cruelty and seeming randomness we both saw in the world. Often, he just smiled a little bit, as I ranted. Other times, he commended a question I had asked, but he might add that "we simply don't know, at least not for certain."

Arthur said he knew most about God from what God had done in his life, not from reading theology. And though he encouraged me to read deeply, it was the blessings he'd experienced during the years he sought faith that convinced him the most. "The hard stuff," he said, "I have to leave to faith."

"To faith, Arthur?" I asked. "Even with your education?"

"Yes, Jim," he said, smiling, "even with *our* education. Or else, what is faith for?"

In time, Arthur gave me my first New Testament—not the whole Bible, mind you, but just the New Testament—in simple-to-understand modern English. I didn't know such versions existed.

"You might want to read this, Jim," he told me.

When I asked him where I might begin, he suggested, "The

Gospels. Any one. But keep your eyes on Jesus. Try to listen to what He says, especially."

I began to read Arthur's little gift and, wonder of wonders, I could understand a surprising amount of what I was reading. But Arthur didn't check up on my progress. He didn't ring my doorbell and hand me a schedule. Once again, he only wanted to be helpful. There were no demands, no begging, just a simple, "Let me know if you'd like to talk about it. I'm sure I could learn a lot from you."

That was the Arthur I came to know. A man who never gave me more than gentle nudges in directions I'll be forever grateful I took. For any more than a gentle nudge was not his way. Always, he merely suggested.

Gradually, I came to rely on his timely, gracious suggestions. Even today, I find myself wondering, "What would Arthur do?"

UNDERSTANDING ARTHUR . . . AND *THE MISSION*

About a year and a half had passed since that eventful *Tres Dias* weekend. In the midst of the hope-filled upheaval my life had become, Arthur and I saw *The Mission,* a film about powerful men and what they would do to get their way.

The Mission tells the sad story of an eighteenth-century tribe of Guarani Indians living deep in the jungles of central South America. Though far removed from us in time and space, their plight connects us, nonetheless, with the sins of big shots, whose cultural religion mixed poisonously with arrogance and greed. In 1750, Spain and Portugal were embroiled in dispute over the borders of what are today Argentina, Paraguay, and Brazil. At stake were much more than boundary lines, however. At stake was the fate of the native Guarani, a people under the protection of Jesuit missionaries.

The Jesuits had nurtured, educated, and evangelized these people, at considerable risk to themselves. But notwithstanding the

Jesuits' protection, some of Europe's most powerful men gathered to settle the disputed boundaries and, along with the borders, the Guarani's fate.

Out of fear, a pliable church bent to the will of the rich and powerful. The Jesuits pleaded for the Guarani, whatever might happen to the boundaries. But the powers of the age—all nominal Christians—overran the mission, exterminating or enslaving the entire Guarani population. The rampaging authority had the full consent of the church.

The film stirred up emotion in me that I hadn't expected.

"How can people act like this, Arthur, if they know God?" I asked, as if we had never seen such behavior before, as if we'd never been part of a power group like those in *The Mission*.

Arthur didn't know what to say, and was quiet a long time. But being with him, I was beginning to feel the previously unknown joys of friendship, even after watching a film about disturbing realities. At least I had someone to talk to, someone with whom I could think out loud. This was new. And it felt very good.

We both knew that the worlds of business and law produced few real friendships. Our worlds were built on competing interests, not friendships. Underneath what seemed like friendship were often convenient alliances forged to get things done, to increase our chances of mutual success. But then if we knew of few friendships, neither did we know of many who sought them. For friendship could be dangerous. Revealing. Entangling. Maybe corrupting, but certainly compromising, for friendship demands vulnerability.

And why would we want to be vulnerable?

I may have been sophisticated in finance, but inside, I was still a little boy. I knew how to look good but far less about being good.

In the world in which Arthur and I spent much of our waking hours, there was plenty of posturing on ethics, at least for our clients. Yet we both knew that at some deeper level, most of us, even those of some faith, remained, somehow, unconverted. Our intellects take in important truth, but our hearts remain stubborn. Intellectually, we know *how* to behave—if things don't get too rough. But if crossed, we fall back on ourselves.

Just like the Spanish and the Portuguese in *The Mission.*

They knew better. They knew how to behave. But if words didn't get what they wanted, they knew how to do "whatever it takes" to get what they wanted.

I knew that drill, too— maybe better than Arthur did.

No, as Arthur and I talked about *The Mission,* it was not for lack of books on ethics or role models, or right-minded New Year's resolutions that left us serving ourselves. Nor was it faulty twelve-step programs or self-improvement schemes or even lack of "good" churches to keep us on track. It was not that we didn't *know,* nor never *knew* about goodness, so much as we kept forgetting. Or, maybe, we never learned to want to do right at a deep enough level.

Maybe it was just never important enough, as important, say, as winning.

Strange, but that Sunday afternoon, after watching *The Mission,* I began to think about sin. Not just other people's sin, but my own. My deep, abiding determination to look out for me. This too was new. I thought about the way I acted at home, the careless, selfish way I loved Lizzie, the indifference I often expressed over our kids' problems. I said, "I'm busy." Or, "I need time for me." But this was only cover for my self-absorption, which is the same sin that flourished in *The Mission,* and will continue to as long as we live in a fallen world. As long as we, consciously or unconsciously, put ourselves ahead of others, sin will flourish like the grass in May. I realized, then, that like my powerful European brothers in *The Mission,* I knew far more about the right things to do than having the will to do them.

"Talking about doing right is the easy part, Jim," Arthur said. "*Doing* is a lot harder, even if, once in a while, it seems easy."

For "the doing," we both knew, is a whole different kettle of fish. It often involves denying our wills. And like many, I was wrestling with "Why do that—what's the need?" But Arthur felt that the "good life" I now sought lay along a path strewn with discipline, humility, and courage, a path that would demand wisdom and—yikes!—something he called *obedience.*

I needed to change, in other words, but I still didn't know how. "We can't *do* what we don't know, nor what we aren't yet," Arthur told me.

I had just begun to understand what that might mean. For unless my heart changed, I'd never do the right thing. Yet even if my heart changed, Arthur was warning me it wouldn't be easy.

As we talked after *The Mission,* he knew I was beginning to read new things and think new thoughts. I even spent a few minutes each morning trying to pray. But still he wanted me to be careful. "It's easy to overestimate the power our actions give us. We think morning devotions will, somehow, keep us from wrong. But it's not that simple. In a fallen world, doing right is hard, even if we have faith. And if we don't think deeply or shrewdly, we'll underestimate, like many do, how easily we lose our way."

I didn't really get—or maybe I didn't want to get—what Arthur was saying. But I knew that just a year before I was certain that a quick divorce was the right thing for me. Why? Because I was unhappy: I didn't always get my way.

Still, this Jesus talk didn't make me comfortable, either. Yet Arthur wanted me to know something Jesus told His own friends: "If you love me, *obey* my commandments."[1] Jesus didn't want His followers thinking that talk was the test. Like us all, they had to learn to *obey*.

"But obey what, Arthur?" I asked, frustrated.

Arthur and I were talking about Jesus. How hard—and strange—me, talking about Jesus! I knew how to speak well, and I knew how to put people on with my talk. I was good with words, and I knew that. I knew their immense power, whether I meant them or not. And I knew how to use words to get my way. But I, like most adults, don't obey very well, unless somehow I've come to believe in someone or something very deeply. Arthur was telling me his Jesus was such a person: "If you love me, *do* what I say."

Arthur's challenge to me to place my faith in something other than me was puzzling. What else was there to place my faith in, other than what I could see and hold? But back then, I was just getting acquainted with spiritual stuff, and how it might apply to my own tangled life. I wanted things to get better for me and my family, and Arthur was trying to convince me that spiritual change was the path along which lay a change for the good. To start on that path, he said, I had to learn to listen and obey. Only then would I choose better. That, he thought, would help me out of my confusion, starting at home. But would it?

By the time I met Arthur, I was already a father to two little boys with whom I spent very little time. I'd wanted to divorce their mother, my wife of thirteen years, even though I'd promised myself I'd never divorce. I came from a broken home myself and said I didn't want to do that to my own kids. But I was about to do just that. At work, I also led people, but rarely thought about their lives. I just wanted them to produce. I was like that in my leadership in my community too. I just wanted people to meet goals, nothing more. Yet I'd been commended for such leadership, even though I had little idea what I wanted from those who followed me, other than good results. I was, underneath, a very troubled soul.

Arthur was teaching me how to lead myself differently, so that, one day, I might lead others better. It was risky, I felt, but he was showing me with his own life that I had to want to do what was right, not just what worked. I was learning, under his patient tutelage, what my fancy college education never taught me: that doing right is fundamentally about doing right for the right reasons. And I was learning, too, that doing that is never easy.

In my business life before knowing Arthur, I was disinclined, for too long, to consider spiritual things. Why? Mostly because of my own selfishness. But also because too many churchgoers I met, whether they were Christians or not, radiated phoniness. One Christian told me as he described some horrible health issues his family was going through, "We just go from victory to victory in the Lord."

"What does going from 'victory to victory' mean?" I asked Arthur, as I recalled the bums lining the corridors at Grand Central Station and homeless mothers with kids along my way to work. Were all these hurting people condemned by God? Didn't God care about them, too?

I got an embarrassed smile, but no answer.

I distrusted anybody's glassy perfection, and thank God, Arthur didn't have that. In fact, until I met Arthur and he told me about his failed marriage and his struggles with his kids and his hope for a purposeful retirement serving others, I thought religion was a crock.

Still today, I distrust the maturity of anyone who tells me Jesus has solved all his problems. But Arthur, the Harvard lawyer on Wall Street, made me willing to listen to a Christian without rolling my eyes.

Too many Christians think—much as the world does—that they have to look like winners to influence people. Too many feel that vulnerability, or transparency, such as Arthur modeled, would be like skin cancer. Worse still, admitting weakness or unresolved personal struggle would be death to them and seemingly to the cause of serving God.

You got to be kidding!

I used to think, right after I came to faith, that Christian business-people had to be different. If someone knew Jesus, I thought, God would put a hedge around that person to keep him from straying. Or, so I thought. Silly me.

So, when I began to care about God myself, I was sure I'd find lots of spiritual people like Arthur, who'd take time to think through important matters. But the more I met religious types, the more they seemed to live like everyone else—within narrow silos of home, work, and play. Just like my New York work buddies, they seemed inclined, first, to protect themselves, their families and what they had and, second, to avoid vulnerability.

Many wanted to retire early and live comfortably. Many chased money as much as my locker room pals. Too many divorced as trivially as my old pals did. Apparently, this was not new. I was at first shocked to read about Daniel Drew, the multimillionaire nineteenth-century business tycoon, who believed he was an outstanding Christian. Though he went bankrupt in 1876 and died three years later, he funded many good projects, including Drew Theological Seminary, in New Jersey, as well as a girls' school in New York. But regardless of what he gave in God's service, he remained a rugged individualist, playing by one set of rules at church, and another at business—just as many spiritually-minded business people do today.

Drew once observed:

> *Sentiment is all right up in that part of the town where your*
> *home is. But downtown, no. Down there, the dog that snaps*
> *the quickest gets the bone. Friendship is very nice for a Sunday*
> *afternoon when you're sitting around the dinner table with*
> *your relations, talking about the sermon that morning. But*
> *nine o'clock Monday morning, [such] notions should be*
> *brushed aside like cobwebs from a machine. I never took any*
> *stock in a man who mixed up business with anything else. He*
> *can go into other things outside of business hours, but when*
> *he's in the office he ought not to have a relation in the world—*
> *and least of all a poor relation.*[2]

Then, too, I remember taking a business trip to Chicago, about six months after I met Arthur. In the suburbs, I met one of my most polite, Christian, Midwestern clients, a man who had, over several years, become a friend (or a "friend" as I would have understood the term in 1986). Not having seen him for perhaps a year, I thought I'd have a lot to share with him. At lunch, after some small talk, I screwed up my courage to tell him, sheepishly, that I thought I'd met God. (I didn't know how to describe it.) I thought, if anyone could, he would understand, and besides, I was far enough away from New York that even if he didn't, the news probably wouldn't reach anyone else. I was excited, if inexperienced, talking about such things. And I thought, of all my buddies, this Midwesterner might understand.

He did. Well, sort of.

He worked for McDonald's. Not flipping burgers, but as an executive at their corporate headquarters in Oak Brook, Illinois. Hearing my confession, he immediately smiled knowingly and nodded his head. Those were good signs, I thought. Then he told me he understood perfectly—an even better sign, I thought. Next, he translated what he'd heard into his own words, and I knew immediately I should have kept my mouth shut.

"Jim," he said, "on Sundays, I honor God, family, and McDonald's—in that order." And then, with a wink, he continued, "On Mondays, I turn my list around."

My friend from Chicago didn't have a clue what Arthur was beginning to unfold to me.

Arthur and I talked about people like Daniel Drew and my McDonald's friend after *The Mission.* As one so new to taking God seriously, I thought if I got my faith "right" from the start the rest would be easy. But while Arthur encouraged me to grow in my faith, he didn't encourage the fantasy that I would always get it right. He didn't believe we're preserved from straying in this fallen world because we have faith.

"You have free will, too, Jim. That's both a gift and a curse. We can try to make a difference," he said. "But it won't be easy, and often, it may cost you."

"Simply to say 'I know Jesus,'" Arthur added, "is not going to make us different. Saying that alone is not going to protect us from temptation, either. My experience in life and my clients' lives prove that."

Notes

1. See John 14:15 NKJV.
2. Daniel Drew, as quoted in Robert Bartels, ed., *Ethics in Business* (Columbus, Ohio: Ohio State Univ., 1963), 35.

GOING DEEPER
WITH ARTHUR . . .
AND LIZZIE

Both life and my own foolishness gnawed at me. I wanted to believe that if I followed God wholeheartedly, life would get easier. But my conversations with Arthur offered little comfort in that area.

"Yes, Jim, God helps us. But it's still our choice. Knowing Him won't keep us from making poor choices. You know, the devil himself can masquerade as 'an angel of light.'"

I suspected Arthur was right. Still, I hoped that trying to live differently I would quickly change into a new person in my home and my life. Arthur promised me God would send grace, something about which I still knew very little. But I had to do my homework too.

During that first year, I continued to ask Arthur some of the crazy questions that have puzzled skeptics and believers for centuries. Old standbys, like, How can there be a God, given the starving children in Africa? Or, Why do bad things happen to good

people? Or, How come so many bad people thrive while the good
die young?

I wonder now why I asked Arthur such questions. I wish it was
because I hungered to know, or that I was willing to learn. But I
doubt that I was. At first, I just may have wanted to show off. I may
have wanted to shock Arthur, if I could. My questions had less to do
with earnest searching (because I wasn't sure there were answers) and
more to do with my daring to be an outspoken agnostic to somebody who had faith. Mainly, I didn't want Arthur to get too close to
me. I didn't want to get into a position where he could hurt me.

And while I never got to revel in his reactions to my edgy sys-
tem of unbelief or my phony courage to live without fairy tales, neither did I get what I expected from Arthur.

What I got, instead, was a smart but humble and fair-minded
human being, a courageous realist, who didn't believe in the Easter
Bunny, after all. He was a gracious man, willing to fence with a cynic.

And because of his intelligence and graciousness, it also didn't
take me long to want to hear him out. I listened, not just because of
his credentials but because his good nature and humility told me I
might learn a lot from listening.

On account of him I overcame my initial prejudice that the Bible
was anything other than a book for losers. Because of him, I started
to read it. But when I began reading Matthew 1 and got bogged
down in that opening genealogy, looking for Jesus (as Arthur had
told me to), I was ready to give up. I told him so, too. But then he
encouraged me to begin with another book. Which I did, and soon,

even though Matthew's opening had tempted me to quit, I started to feel the strange power Scripture exerts, if we give it a chance.

So I skipped to the gospel of John. And after that, I bounced around the New Testament. In time, I landed in Paul's "letter to the Romans," for no better reason than that, once on a business trip, I'd stopped off in Rome. I didn't know places like Corinth or Philippi, but I had been to Rome. I wondered what this guy Paul, about whom I knew nothing, had to say about Rome or to the Romans. I think I expected a travelogue. I wondered if Paul might have seen some of the same sights I had. But long before I got to the letter's seventh chapter, without a hint of the Coliseum or the Appian Way, I knew this wasn't *National Geographic.* I felt as if Paul were writing to me personally.

> *I do not understand what I do. . . . I have the desire to do*
> *what is good, but I cannot carry it out. For what I do is not*
> *the good I want to do; no, the evil I do not want to do—this I*
> *keep on doing. . . . When I want to do good, evil is right there*
> *with me. . . . What a wretched man I am!*[1]

When I read those words for the first time, I had to put the book down. I was dumbstruck. I read the words again. These words were written to me. And like Arthur, I sensed Paul was going out of his way to say something very helpful to me, based on hard-won wisdom or maybe a gift from heaven. He was taking a risk saying what he did. Like Arthur did. As if Paul, like Arthur, had thought long and hard about who I was and had considered my screwiness and the person I was becoming, and then sat down to write me a letter challenging my thinking. Paul asked me what—because of Arthur—I was already only beginning to ask myself:

"Why do you do the things that you do, Jim? And why don't you do the things you know you ought to do?"

Before I met Arthur, in some screwy way I knew I loved Lizzie. But I also wanted to control her in destructive ways, too, and I felt powerless to change. I thought I worked hard and brought home a good life for my family, and I expected Lizzie to be glad to see me. I expected her to be eager to spend time with me, even to wait on me. But with the serious challenges our oldest son presented Lizzie, especially at that time, she wasn't in the mood and often chose to go out at night. Not to bowl, or to Tupperware parties, but to school board meetings and citizens' groups that were trying to help kids with special needs. Though our son was born to both Lizzie and me, I shared little of her deep passion for his well-being. Nurture I left to Lizzie.

Her obsession with our Nicky led me to accuse her, increasingly, of failing me as my wife. That hurt her, and I knew it. So, in my twisted economy of married life, I wanted to hurt Lizzie, and possibly Nicky, because I felt unhappy.

Or, so it seemed at the time. And this is who I was when I first met Arthur, on my way to divorce.

My attitudes were sometimes destructive to Lizzie, and to our marriage. But I didn't seem to care, and even when I did, I felt both unable and unwilling to change. Meeting Arthur didn't change me overnight, of course. But meeting him and learning from him began to change my environment enough that, in time, I began to hear the Someone who could change me.

Arthur, remember, was the one who had suggested I go on that three-day retreat in Connecticut in late April 1985. I did, of course, and found it deeply affecting. But I didn't know if what touched me was real or just a temporary aftereffect from being around a bunch of nice men for a weekend. Had my weekend been affected . . . or had my life? It would take time to know. But I was hopeful.

I didn't wait too long before my first test and an answer. On Tuesday, April 30, 1985, Lizzie came upstairs in our lovely home to tell me, yet again, that she was going out that night to another board of education meeting. By then, the poor woman must have been weary from the delicate struggle to find words that didn't detonate an explosion. It couldn't have been easy. She tiptoed into our library and asked "if it would be all right?"

That question was rhetorical, I'd long felt. She knew it was never all right, but she'd go anyway. "So why even ask?" I used to think. In the past, I greeted this ritual dishonesty with sarcasm and anger. But now just two days after the weekend that had shaken awake some inner deadness, two days after I had begun to pray that, somehow, I might really begin to be different, I had an opportunity to show Lizzie what God can do, through conversations with a friend.

For two days, I had been praying, as best as I knew how, that God would help me understand how I needed to change. What was I to do now? Was I—I hoped—like the Ebenezer Scrooge of the "morning after," having seen the ghosts of the past, present, and future, and been given a second chance? Or was I the same clown I'd been for years?

I didn't know. But I knew, with granite certainty, that whatever the weekend meant, if it didn't change my relationship with Lizzie, it was meaningless self-deception. In fact, since I believed I'd actually met God that weekend and experienced His forgiveness and love, I knew that if I had, it was so that I would "go and do likewise," that I might better love and forgive others in return. And it was Lizzie in particular to whom I felt specially directed to go first with this new understanding.

So that Tuesday night might be the very dawn of my new life, and if it was, I was not going to miss the opportunity to become a new creation.[2] That very moment, on that Tuesday night in April when Lizzie asked me again if I minded her going out, was really another gift. For it gave me my first, real opportunity since coming back home to show her how sorry I was for the many times I had made her feel lousy when all she wanted to do was help our son.

I jumped up from my desk and I hugged her and told her, "Have a great time, and don't worry about when you get home."

Hearing me say that, she drew back slowly. Looking puzzled, she asked me, "Are you feeling OK?"

I told her I was. At the very least, I hoped she might understand that, over the weekend, I had a vision—if only that—of the husband and father I one day would be. And with God's help—and

Arthur's friendship—it just might happen. But it would take time, and I hoped Lizzie would have patience with me.

When Lizzie came home at about 10:30 that night, I was already in bed, trying to sleep. But this time, I really was trying, not just feigning sleep in order to waylay Lizzie in the dark lateness, after her return from trying to help our boy. Over the years, you see, I had honed my awful skills in imposing the maximum degree of pain on Lizzie while never laying a hand on her. For at just such a moment, as when Lizzie returned from a meeting and had washed up and was about to get into bed, I would fly into a rage. And though I had never been able to keep Lizzie from going to her "stupid" meetings, I could, and did—too often—practice my ugly drill on her once she got back. It was a mean and destructive payback for having left me that night.

Amazingly, after enduring all these scary scenes, Lizzie loved me and hated to fight, especially late at night. The fights kept her awake longer, and more often, than they did me. I knew that, and I picked just such moments to rip into her to hurt her deliberately. I'd tell her she was coming home too late, wasn't caring about me, thinking only about herself and the kids; even telling her, directly and indirectly, she was being a lousy wife.

Lizzie had put up pathetic defenses before my onslaughts. She knew that, if I was awake (which I typically was) that she'd catch hell from me. But if I wasn't, then, whew! she'd made it—at least that night. But she hated to fight, and I knew that.

So, she had worked it out, over time, that upon getting home, she'd sneak into our bedroom, quietly open her dresser, and reach for her nightgown. Then she'd slip into the bathroom, close the door, turn on the light, wash and change, turn out the light, and then hope to get into her side of our bed without waking the monster who slept next to her.

Well, that Tuesday night I was still awake when Lizzie came home. But through the grace of God, and probably the prayers of Arthur, I didn't erupt. I simply asked Lizzie, in the dark, after she was in bed, whether she had had a good meeting.

My question must have shocked her: She sat bolt upright in bed and turned on the light.

"What has happened to you?" she demanded. She seemed more scared by the fact I was different—early as this was—than that I would rail against her again. She didn't consider that I had begun to change for the better. It was just too early.

"I don't know," I said. But I hoped whatever it was, it would be real and permanent. I told her again that I wanted to become a better husband and father than I'd been. And, once more, I told her I was sorry for the pain I had caused her over the years.

I also told her I loved her.

I'm not sure Lizzie slept any better that night than in the past when I tried to hurt her. But this time, I didn't intend to keep her awake. I think Lizzie knew that too. A change had begun—just begun—to come over me, a change that, like the leaves on the trees that spring, could not, I hoped, be stopped.

Arthur set something in motion, new and sometimes bewildering. But it would be good and life-giving. I could already see that. Lizzie could see it too. And this was how I wanted to live from now on. Arthur's friendship had opened a way of life to me that I first thought was only possible for Trappist monks or poets. Before it had seemed irrelevant to me. Only with Arthur did I begin to explore the merest possibility that there was something in that life that I might desire.

* * *

Our friendship would continue face-to-face for five years. Then, in 1989, four years after Arthur introduced me to the courtesy and patience of Jesus, I moved away from our comfortable New York suburb to a bigger and better-paying job in Boston.

As we prepared to part, I felt torn. Here was the best—and the first—friend I'd ever had in my adult life and for nothing more than a bigger job and more money, I was leaving. Here, too, was the father I had always wanted. Here was the man who introduced me to God, and the man who, more than anyone else in the world, changed my cynical, selfish view of the world. He helped save my marriage and save me from ruining my family. He had given me hope when I so desperately needed it, not knowing I did.

And now I was leaving for Boston. Was it really worth it, I wondered. Or was I still just as crazy as I had long been? As we stood in my doorway for the last time, I mumbled a few words of intense gratitude and hugged Arthur. Graciously, he told me, "Don't look back. Just look ahead."

Ahead, in five years, I would be out of the money management business altogether and into the college classroom, where I would teach business and economics at a small college in Indiana. Ahead, too, in late 1994, my Lizzie, with whom I had fallen in love all over again, would be diagnosed with terminal breast cancer. Together, Lizzie and I—with the comfort of a gracious God I was just beginning to know—would face down that monster. But would we ever have—or would I have even been with Lizzie during her hour of need—had I never known Arthur?

Ahead, Lizzie and I would walk through the fires of hell together and be among the lucky few to come through the horror together. We would survive her cancer treatments, her heart failure, her heart transplant, lung problems, kidney failure and much, much more. And we'd come through more dedicated to each other and to serving others in spite of—or maybe because of—the pain we had endured. But would I have been willing to face the pain, had I never met Arthur?

In retrospect, five years of conversations with Arthur had prepared me well, or as well as one can be for the severe challenges ahead. I did not know how harshly Lizzie and I would be tested. But Arthur had encouraged me to face life's painful realities, to grow as a human being, not just as a business executive, and not just as a person of faith, either. He wanted my faith to spread into every nook and cranny of my life. He wanted to challenge and stretch my values. The "old me," who, for so long, thought money and networking would be enough for whatever was ahead, never would have withstood the strains that awaited us in 1994, and have followed us ever since.

I had risen to be an executive with some of the world's finest investment firms, but in fighting for my Lizzie's life, in struggling to be faithful to her, and to my commitments to God, the struggles I'd had in business seemed as so much child's play.

Because of Arthur's friendship, Lizzie and I left the empty beauty of suburban life to explore a life of meaningful service to others. Through our unexpected friendship, my dying love for Lizzie was resurrected, like irises in spring. In place of weariness with Lizzie, even when things were good, I was given a new, fulfilling relationship with her—even as she, only in her early forties, was being taken apart, brick by brick, by cancer. Our children too (now three of them) were touched by Arthur, who so hoped to be a grandfather they never had. They were raised by a more caring dad because Arthur had touched me.

But it all began with Arthur. For it was he who started me down a path that would prepare me for the most important work of my life—caring for Lizzie and teaching college—redemptive works that, I hope, will touch others, as Arthur had touched me. It was he, after all, who had reached me by going deep, by being humble, by daring to be intimate, by challenging my thinking. And by encouraging me to go and do likewise.

Notes

1. Romans 7:15, 18–19, 21, 24.

2. The Bible describes a follower of Jesus as being a "new creation" (2 Corinthians 5:17).

SEVEN

LEARNING TO LOVE LIZZIE . . . ANEW

Arthur affected my life profoundly in many ways, but at the beginning, it was clearly in my life with Lizzie where I felt his first influence. Marriage and family were my Normandy beaches that, seemingly, had to be retaken from the forces of darkness before any liberation army could come ashore.

I'm not one to blame my parents, or anyone else, for who I had become. But in my early life I had seen few models of loving interaction between a man and a woman. In marriage, I assumed you got what you could get away with.

At worst, that meant you might hurt someone you said you loved.

I'd been effective getting what I wanted. But pushiness rarely worked with my wife, who, before my demands, was simply overwhelmed. For the woman I married is not only different from me because she is a woman but because she is a nicer person. For she cared about other people, whereas I didn't. Unless they could do something for me.

The Lizzie I met in 1967 backstage at a play and whom I married in 1971 was the most beautiful girl I'd ever met in my life. For a long, long time, I didn't understand the gift she is—until, that is, it was almost too late. I still don't always appreciate the gifts I get, but who does?

Lizzie's quiet, and I'm gregarious—even loud at times, as my father was. She's gentle; I'm assertive. She accommodates, avoids confrontation; I'm willful, even combative. A psychologist friend of ours told us that in marriage there's often a "distancer" and a "pursuer." As life stresses us, the distancer seeks "space" to think things through. The distancer tries to escape, to think, and finally, to talk . . . later (maybe). But the pursuer wants the opposite. The pursuer wants to talk RIGHT NOW! And even though she—or he—may realize that talking won't provide a quick fix, the pursuer still finds just talking to be helpful.

But the distancer sees things differently. He believes the pursuer's desire "just to talk" is unnecessary and dangerous, even inconsiderate, so he distances still more. On and on this destructive dance goes. In this devilish cycle, the pursuer hounds the distancer, while the distancer abandons the pursuer. Or so it seems to each. Communication breaks down amid anger and tears, and stress only escalates.

Usually, our therapist friend told us, it's the guy who's the distancer and the woman who's the pursuer. She wants to talk; he wants to watch "the game." Well, surprisingly, as a male, I'm the pursuer in our marriage; Lizzie is the distancer. If you think of guys who'd rather play a video game than talk to their wives, that was not me. If you think of a young mother desperate for an adult conversation, especially with someone she loves, after spending the day with the kids, that was not the case in our house! No way, Jose! Any night, this guy would have rather talked to his Lizzie until four o'clock in the morning about her bad day, or about building her a greenhouse than have watched a close World Series game.

Kind of strange, no? But put the tools and the temperament of a pursuer into a male, and the humor quickly can fade. And, in our house, it frequently did.

Not that we fought in public. Oh, no. We weren't that kind of couple. But just below the surface of our lives was a boiling cauldron of frustration, desire, and fear. We both hurt. For different reasons, of course. I, for loneliness and for being rebuffed for wanting to get closer to the woman I loved, and Lizzie, scared and feeling like a failure for not "measuring up" to my demands. We were both stuck —loving each other, yes, but doing so in dangerous ways. Which of us felt more pain, or who hurt the other more deeply through sins of commission or omission, I don't know. It's no longer important, either. But such memories still eat at me, reminding me of the painful misuse of the gift I was given in Lizzie.

As a consequence of the struggles Lizzie and I shared with each other, as well as raising a child with special needs, we often felt the sting of each other's faintest criticism. For life—for both of us—was not what we had hoped. We looked great, but few knew how fragile we had become.

This is who I was when I met Arthur. I was someone who could suit up well and make a great impression. But if you crossed me, hold your hat. If maturity may be defined as our ability to tolerate pain, then I was a child.

As a business executive, I was very familiar with the important difference between having a good idea and executing it. Execution is the real test. Winners know how to execute. At work, I was a winner who knew how to execute. Colleges are full of professors with lots of good ideas that will never get executed. But good businesspeople know how to execute. At least at work they do. They're paid big money when they execute well. At home, however, where I also had significant investments, I couldn't execute good ideas for squat, even if I had them, or for the love of Lizzie, whom I kept hurting over and over.

Arthur's surgical tools began to reach parts of me that caused so much intended and unintended mischief, cutting here, making a new connection there. How is still a mystery to me, yet I know he was one of God's special tools sent to me. He was my mountain come to Muhammad, so to speak, because this Muhammad was not willing to go to any mountain, even if a mountaintop experience awaited me.

Little by little, because of the way Arthur unpacked truth so that I might hear it, I began to change. Step by little step. But as I look back, I'm not sure I *wanted* to change at first. I certainly didn't think I needed to. Yes, I knew I had conflicts at home, and, yes, some of them were probably my own making. But like the Irish mother watching her gawky son in a parade, I thought to myself, "They're all out of step but my boy Jimmy." So too with me. It was everyone else who was screwed up.

I was convinced that Lizzie had the major problems requiring immediate fixing: poor time management, moodiness, the overall lack of productive output and, of course, lack of appreciation of the hero she had in me. These were major things to be wrong with somebody. And Lizzie rarely seemed, at the time, serious about fixing her own big problems.

Again, it was all those others, including Lizzie, who gave me a hard time. It was *they* who were screwed up. I was not the kind of person to cause problems for anyone who had their heads screwed on straight. And I surely didn't need any major fixing up.

C. S. Lewis, whom I'd later read voraciously, had a wonderful picture of where I probably was when Arthur came into my life:

> *Imagine yourself as a living house. God comes in to rebuild that house. At first, perhaps, you can understand what He is doing. He is getting the drains right and stopping the leaks in the roof and so on. . . . But presently He starts knocking the house about in a way that hurts abominably and does not seem to make sense. What on earth is He up to? He is building quite a different house from the one you thought of— throwing out a new wing here, putting up towers, making*

courtyards. You thought you were going to be made into
a decent little cottage: but He is building a palace.
He intends to live in it Himself.[1]

That's probably where I was in February 1985, when Arthur first suggested I "might like to go" on a three-day retreat like one that had impacted his own life. So, fearful but hopeful, a few weeks later, I went.

I had no idea what was in store for me.

You read about it briefly in chapter 4. Now here's my response to the *Tres Dias* retreat: It felt somewhat like hitting a wall at 80 mph. So powerful was it that, afterward, I, who often used words to make my living, found myself dumbfounded trying to describe what happened. The closest I got were Blaise Pascal's words. Pascal, a seventeenth-century mathematical genius, happened to meet God also unexpectedly one night:

The year of grace 1654,
Monday, 23 November, Feast of St. Clement, Pope and martyr . . .
From about half-past ten in the evening until half-past midnight,
FIRE
God of Abraham, God of Isaac, God of Jacob,
not of philosophers and scholars,
Certainty, certainty, heartfelt, joy, peace.
God of Jesus Christ . . .
My God and your God,

"Thy God shall be my God."
The world forgotten, and everything except God. . . .
Joy, joy, joy, tears of joy
I have cut myself off from Him. . . .
Let me not be cut off from Him forever!
"And this is life eternal, that they might
know Thee, the only true God, and Jesus
Christ Whom Thou hast sent."
Jesus Christ.
Jesus Christ.[2]

Pascal was onto something. In Connecticut, something very powerful had happened. As Arthur drove me home that night from our *Tres Dias* encounter, I wanted so much to share that something with Lizzie, along with the hope I also felt that things would change for us. But once home, words failed me. Utterly. I couldn't control my emotions. I was shocked by the person I'd been for years, and by what I had intended to do—divorce Lizzie. And then, I felt that God stooped, even for the likes of me.

When I saw Lizzie, I cried. I told her I was sorry. Very sorry. And that I felt I was, with God's help, going to become a very different husband to her and father to our children.

Lizzie didn't know what to say, given the mess I must have appeared.

"Have you gone out of your mind?" she later told me was one question she had. Another was if I might be using a "religious experience" as my ticket out of our marriage, since I'd threatened to leave so many times before. Still another thought was, "given his genetic material, maybe he's snapped like his mother."

But if my emotions seemed, like Pascal's, a bit over the top, by the next weekend, Pascal's words were still about the best I could find. Yet, I felt an overwhelming need to try to fathom what had happened to me on that weekend. I wanted to say something, because there was a fire burning within me that had to come out.

Don, that pastor I'd berated in my "welcome to town" speech, the same guy who first invited me to that Sunday morning men's prayer group which I now attended regularly, challenged me to say a few words in church the next Sunday, April 28, 1985. I said I'd try. It was those very remarks, in fact, that I was working on when Lizzie came into our library the Tuesday night after my weekend to tell me she was going out to a board of education meeting. (You read about my reaction in the previous chapter.)

That next Sunday, I went up into a church pulpit to speak for the first time in my life. It was my very first public witness, and I as unlikely a witness as there could ever be. I had been pulled through a knothole the size of a Cheerio by the love of God and a friend named Arthur. It was exactly seven days since I'd come home from the retreat.

"Good morning," I began. "As some of you may know, last weekend three of us were away at a monastery in New Canaan, Connecticut, for a three-day experience in living the Christian life called 'Tres Dias.' We arrived Thursday night. And I must admit to a certain apprehension about being in a monastery, especially without a car. I'd never been in a real monastery before, and the thought of the three days ahead seemed like an awful lot of unsampled food to have heaped upon my plate. 'Uh-oh,' I thought. 'This is a mistake.'

"I'd heard about these kinds of things; you know . . . for religious fanatics! And while I had been curious when first invited to go, now, I was scared. Would I find wild-eyed, Bible-toting, Bible-quoting, true-believer fanatics speaking to each other of their mystical experiences? Or, maybe, find crazies and zanies saying absolutely nothing sensible to those, like me, still on the far side of paradise? I was very worried. In fact, I was intimidated. Especially since I didn't have a car.

"Then, too, I worried about my freedom. For, as unlikely as it might be, just suppose—suppose, mind you—something really *did* happen to me while I was away. You know, suppose I had one of those experiences we hear about once in a while. What if, say, I came to see *the* light—or *any* light? What would happen to me? Would my life shrivel up? Would the fun this world holds for me, and which I'd come to like—and really didn't want to change, sinful or not—be squeezed out of me?

"While I have always been a curious human being—sometimes too much so—this time I thought I just may have gotten in over my head. There I was, in a monastery. Nighttime. Three days to go. Strangers. Maybe weirdos. Dropped off in another world.

"And no car.

"And what another world it turned out to be!

"For my three days away turned out to be not a retreat but a revelation of an absolutely different world: a world of infinite and indescribable beauty, a world where I think I actually met God. And God turned out to be love."

I looked up from my notes and gazed at the audience, knowing how these words must have sounded, spoken by one of their own, an irregular, uncommitted churchgoer until a week before. A few smiled. One or two women had damp eyes, clearly moved by what they were hearing. Others, especially several men I knew, seemed impatient, maybe angry.

"Now, lest I sound like the lunatic or the raving maniac I dreaded meeting on the weekend, let me assure you, I still live at home with my family; still go to work; and still, regrettable or not, love a good, dirty joke. And nowhere, in anything I'm saying, am I even hinting at some kind of moral perfection or superiority.

"I don't know why I should have been picked to go on this retreat or to have been touched through it so deeply. Yes, I confess, that sometimes I've sought truth, as many of us have, at different points in their lives. But, in no way was I prepared, nor would I have ever thought, that down a quiet road in New Canaan, Connecticut, I'd meet God Almighty and stand in His presence for a weekend.

"Invisibly, yet lovingly, through the tenderness of others—people who looked just like you and me—God touched me and told me, 'Everything will be all right. Fear nothing.'

"I still have bills to pay, a job to go to, a house to help run, a life to lead, children to help raise, a future to help shape, but 'everything will be all right.'

"That was the message: 'Everything will be all right.'

"Why was I chosen to go on this thing? And why, through it, was I touched so deeply?

"I don't know.

"But I can't ever imagine looking at life as I used to. Everything now seems like a miracle. You and me. Our spring day. The flowers. Our church. Shoes. Toys. Wheelbarrows. Everything! Everything has become a miracle.

"For I have seen the face of God. And He looks exactly like you and me. He blesses you. And loves you too. And longs to bring peace and joy to your life."

As I sat down, I realized that to some I must have sounded as though I'd returned from another planet. Or maybe, from heaven itself. But for me, life now seemed radically different.

It was as if five hundred pounds of weed killer had been dropped on the garden of my soul, killing every weed that grew there. At least for now.

But we must be careful not to confuse surface change with deep change.

Still, that first April—April of 1985—was an extraordinary gift to me, and to Lizzie too. But beyond Lizzie, I was beginning to sense a concern for other human beings that I'd never felt before. A kernel of an idea had been born, that other people were, like me, image bearers of God and entitled to dignity. Just as I was.

Imagine that!

I remember helping a woman who was upset on a subway plat-form in New York City. She was confused about the right train to take. I approached her and offered to help make sure she got the right train. At work, I had a new freedom from worry about "hitting my numbers." Oh, I still had to hit them, but the fear of failure I seemed to carry within my outwardly effortless confidence had lifted. I stopped to talk with "little people" at work.

This was all different. One night at home that week, with spring in full bloom, I asked Lizzie if she'd like to go for a walk. That spring evening I sensed a new and intense beauty in the physical world. This, too, was new. It was the first time in my life, I think, I really saw flowers, greening grass, and budding leaves as gifts too. I'd never experienced this before. I'd never looked so hard on a walk before.

Yet, what I was most grateful for was the new power I was be-ginning to sense over choosing to do right in my relationship with Lizzie. That new power might just begin to help me forge a different kind of relationship with her, a more loving, less demanding, less controlling one.

Vividly, I still remember many of the problems Lizzie and I slogged through during the first fourteen years of our marriage, those rough years before I came to faith. Many of those problems were serious enough that we might have divorced. One of our great-est struggles was in the bedroom.

If I had a bad day at work, I had no problem closing the door of my office, catching a train home, having dinner, playing with the kids, and then, best of all, hoping to hop in bed with Lizzie. For me, a roll in the hay was a surefire way to put a bad day behind me. For me, it was, in fact, far better than a stiff drink.

But I had to come to faith to understand that women are different, most times. If Lizzie heard I'd had a bad day and now wanted to hop in bed, she thought I was a wacko. "How can you possibly do that?" she marveled.

As a woman, her life was cut from a single cloth. If she had a problem with a child in the morning, that problem lingered, stuck to her like a staticky skirt all day and on into the night. If she didn't tell me about the problem, which was often her way, I'd be left wondering about her mood: Was she mad at me? But if I winked at her at dinner after learning she'd had a punky day, and asked her, with the kids looking on, "How 'bout going upstairs?" she might blow her top.

"You just don't understand!" she'd cry.

"What's to understand?" I'd mutter, playing dumb.

Life, to me, was a house of many rooms with doors that closed and locked firmly. A problem in one room did not have to be a problem throughout the house. When a problem arose, most times I could easily walk out of one room, close the door behind me, and go elsewhere, where things might be a lot better. Or at least different. Like the bedroom, with Lizzie.

But for Lizzie—and I now know for most women—her internal house is like an open classroom. There are no doors, locks, or even walls. Everything flows together. The noise and tumult of one stormy area affects everywhere else.

Today, I understand that difference between men and women, between Lizzie and me much better, and I don't assume everybody is wired like me.

But for years before Arthur, I was sure that in my marriage I was right and Lizzie must be wrong. She was just being obstinate. And my job, as I saw it back then, was to show her who ruled the roost, to make her into a normal human being who reacted to stress and thought as I did.

Sound idiotic? Well, twenty years ago, it seemed perfectly natural to me. For how could anyone not want to roll in the hay when things elsewhere go crazy?

In my obtuseness, I couldn't understand that Lizzie might just want to talk or maybe be held. That was OK with me too, up to a point. But only up to a point. For beyond a few minutes of hugging and talking, only a roll in the hay, to me, made sense. To me, that is. And any other point of view besides mine didn't matter, anyway. Important, sensitive matters like these, between the woman I claimed I loved and me, were not open to debate. What had I to learn? And what was there to change? I was perfect already. And if I was perfect, that meant that whatever problems Lizzie and I had were all hers.

"Who knows?" Arthur surprised me, recalling the harm I had done to Lizzie. "Maybe God used your frustration to bring you closer to Him." Surely, later on, when Lizzie was stricken with advanced cancer, I prayed to God that He would help me be faithful, whatever was ahead. For Arthur helped me see that suffering was common to human life, and maturity helped us face it.

After returning from my weekend away, setbacks would occur in the weeks and months to come. However, my life with Lizzie and our children did begin to change for the better. So did my growing concern for others. I began to turn a corner after that April weekend, even if growth was, at times, fitful. Even now, two decades later, I still stumble. I regress under pressure. I still can confuse conversion with transformation. But don't we all, if we're honest? Even those, unlike me, who by nature are like Arthur, gentler people, naturally inclined to live peacefully with others?

Nonetheless, like a graph of long-term returns from stocks I knew and followed, my trend, from the time I met Arthur, began to point upward—toward becoming a more loving, more forgiving human being. I began to forgive others. And even myself.

Martin Luther said, we "carry the nails in our pockets." Every day. And, given what I did to my Lizzie, I will always remember that. But because I met Arthur, a new creation began to grow in me.

That new life would not guarantee I would get my way or that life could not get very hard. And Arthur wanted me to remember those truths too.

In the years since my fateful weekend in Connecticut and since meeting Arthur, I've recalled Arthur's warning at some terrible times of challenge and loss.

My Lizzie has battled life-threatening disease. And during the

struggle to save her life, we've met scores of families in hospital waiting rooms facing similar struggles. One family stands out as particularly tragic. Not because their loved one died (which she did) while
Lizzie hasn't. No, this other family's story is tragic because a husband tried to control what was never his, ultimately, to control.

For Bill loved his Sharon (their names are changed) every bit as
much as I loved my Lizzie. But funny thing, as a believer in God,
too, Bill thought he had the silver bullet. He thought that either
Sharon's doctors had answers to her horrible set of medical issues or,
should they fail, God would pull a rabbit out of a hat—on com-
mand. But, sadly, medical reality doesn't work like that. It doesn't
bend to our wills any more than business does, even if we know
God. Oh, sometimes it will, but not every time. Because we don't
control this life.

Yes, we can, in many cases, influence events. And our faith may
witness a miracle unfold before us. But in the end, neither events—
nor life—is under our control.

Nor is God under our control, however much we may believe
our cause is right and good.

Sharon died. And Bill went to pieces. He blamed the "stupid
doctors" first, and then he blamed God. And then he blamed me,
because his Sharon died and Lizzie lived. His grief grew so large it
twisted his mind to think he should now die. He said he heard
Sharon telling him so . . . or so he thought. He was going to eat bad
stuff, not take medicines he needed, he said crazily to me. And by

golly, he explained, he was going to kill himself, and go be with Sharon, who was calling him from heaven.

The more I questioned him (Bill had a PhD in psychology, by the way), the less he wanted anything to do with me, though we'd been friends for years before Sharon died. Bill stopped returning my phone calls and wouldn't see me. He raged against God because He'd listened to my prayers but not to his. Bill's case is an extreme, of how hard life can get, how confusing, but only in its details.

In New York, an important client of mine was going to have his way too. Dan was a rich and good man. He was a man to whom I became a friend, not just a money manager. At first Dan wanted only to help his beloved daughter and her husband get through the financial pain of his dental school education. Once through school, this good dad set them up in the San Francisco area, where his son-in-law had studied, with a new house and a well-equipped dental office.

But, no sooner had the pictures been hung in the couple's new home, than Dan's little girl flew back to Daddy and cried her eyes out. Deeply distraught, she told Mom and Dad she was getting a divorce. Ashamed, the heartbroken young woman told her loving parents her husband was gay. Her husband had told her he had to follow his heart. Evidently, or so he also told her, the young husband had tried for years to fight his sexuality—tried to deny it too, he told Dan's daughter, but it was no use. He had to get out of the marriage to live with his lover—with a new house, his schooling paid for, and an office set up, all paid by my friend Dan.

Dan was both sad and furious. But he was not going to drown in sorrow. No, even now he was going to take charge. Sitting in my office, he told me he was going to use his assets—and he had plenty —to destroy the young dentist, "even kill him, if necessary." That would be his life's new goal.

My friend Dan was, as I say, a good man. He had lots of good values, but, like my friend Bill, life had overwhelmed him. The control he thought he had over life, if only he acted well, had failed him. It had let him down. In Bill's case, God had also let him down. How much these two good men, and so many others I've met along the way, might have gained by having a friend like Arthur. How much I wish they had met such a friend, and, in meeting such a friend, then had risked letting their Arthur know them.

Deeply.

For through such a friend, they might have met the living God.

Notes

1. C. S. Lewis, quoting a parable by George MacDonald in *Mere Christianity* (San Francisco: HarperCollins, 2001), 205

2. The "Memorial," in Blaise Pascal, *Pensées,* ed. Louis Lafuma, trans. John Warrington (New York: Dutton, 1966), 309. Pascal's quotation "And this is life eternal, that they might know Thee, the only true God, and Jesus Christ Whom Thou hast sent" are from the words of Jesus in John 17:3 (KJV).

ARTHUR'S
THREE QUESTIONS

In 1987, the stock market soared. Lots of newly-minted college grads had been lured to "The Street." Not to pound the pavement, but to work on deals that added up in billions of dollars and fantasize about what they would do with their millions in commissions. Veterans my age, in their thirties and forties, thought about early retirement. One Sunday, when everything seemed to be going so well, *The New York Times* ran a tongue-in-cheek business piece about how hard it can be to live on $600,000 a year.

The market peaked on August 25, and then began a scary, two-month swoon. Finally, on Monday, October 19, it collapsed. U.S. stocks lost almost a quarter of their entire value in a single day—almost a third of their entire worth from a week before.

For those of us watching the tape that day, it was breathtaking and terrifying. The young turks, who, just two months ago, had been counting on making millions, or my own cohorts, who had been planning early retirement on their yachts, turned ashen. Summer giddiness morphed into white-knuckle fear. Our big jobs and hefty bonuses might vanish, along with making the house payment.

By then, I'd known Arthur about two years. I had also grown a bit in my faith—a little bit. Beyond the healing changes that had begun to touch Lizzie and me, the crash put me to a different test, one in which I was trying, however imperfectly, to trust in Someone else. For me, who loved money, this was a big test. However, if I claimed the 1987 financial earthquake didn't scare me, I'd be a lying clown. Because it rocked me—a lot!

Yet Arthur and I were both by then very successful people. I was a senior vice president at a major, New York-based, multinational bank. In spite of the crash, I was still making more money than I ever would have imagined in the early 1970s, when I was a high school teacher satisfied with $7,100 a year. I hadn't aspired to be rich, yet I'd become rich; more because I happened to be in the right place at the right time than because I was a genius. But now, with my riches under daily pressure, my portfolio shrinking by the minute, I thought of little else but money.

Arthur, too, was successful. Unlike me, though, he'd grown up well-off. His father had been born poor, but got a scholarship to Harvard and became a world-renowned maritime lawyer. Arthur was the good son who followed in Dad's footsteps, entered Dad's firm, and grew up to be a respectable lawyer like his father. Not so for me. I was a rebel, inclined to do just the opposite of my father.

But the swooning of our fortunes in the fall of '87 shook us both.

We thought a lot and talked often about money and security. Market events—the real world, that is—forced us, as it often does, to ask ourselves hard questions about life and what we really wanted out of it.

Arthur, like me, was heavily in the market. But unlike me, though close to retirement, he seemed less gripped by unfolding events than I was. I thought my concern might be connected to our two young children. Providing for them, and for Lizzie, spread before me like a walk across America. I wasn't able to walk away from my job. Arthur could, I thought. Yet was retirement the best time for his portfolio to take a big hit? I knew I was only rationalizing; my misery needed company, even though I knew my companion didn't share those thoughts and might retire at any moment.

Except for Arthur, I didn't have anyone to share my fears with—if I admitted them to anyone. Certainly I didn't feel I could reveal my fears to Lizzie.

But Arthur didn't seem to understand.

One ride home in November, as the early-evening darkness of late fall enveloped our train, and our faces reflected off the windows, he said I looked troubled.

"Who, me? Oh, I'm fine, Arthur." But he didn't buy my line.

"Making it is meaningless, Jim, without a higher purpose. You know that."

"But Arthur," I protested, "you're forgetting. You don't have young kids to raise any more and send to college."

More important to me, perhaps, though not said to Arthur, business was a way for me to keep score. Keep score, that is, as in a game I'd long been winning big-time. Until this fall. For a guy like me, who loved to hit his goals, business gave me a stadium in which to show off, to do deals, make money, and win.

But Arthur thought that, without a higher purpose, business people who say they love God can, unwittingly, become captives of opposite worlds; one, a luxuriant, self-deceiving dream, the other, a commitment to eternal values.

"You need to have a higher purpose."

"Maybe so, Arthur. But don't you think, if we are supposed to have higher purpose, then we should have a little gizmo that shows us what real success looks like from 40,000 feet up . . . or from our deathbeds? To help us see reality?"

For, I thought, from 40,000 feet we'd get a heavenly view, the "big picture." Or, if from our deathbeds, we'd get a better understanding of what's truly important. Either way, we'd have a better picture of life than what we have now. Then just maybe, we'd see how trivial stuff gets overrated in importance, while real gifts of everyday life so easily get ignored.

Arthur shared a metaphor of life from Ben Franklin that made me think. Evidently, Franklin saw life like an antique shop full of treasures and junk. But, overnight, some joker broke in and switched the price tags. The valuable was tagged as junk; the worthless was repriced as treasure.

"If we only could see life from that perspective—or from 40,000 feet up or from your deathbed, as you say—maybe we'd see success differently."

Arthur told me another Ben Franklin story I'll also never forget. Seems, growing up, Ben wanted a tin whistle that belonged to another boy. He wanted it so badly he would do almost anything to get it. Its owner, however, wouldn't part with it. He wouldn't, that is, until Franklin offered him a dollar—an outrageous sum of money for an eighteenth-century child to have. But that was what it took to get Ben his whistle! Only problem was, within minutes, Ben knew he'd paid too much for a whistle.

Isn't that our problem too? We pay too much for our whistles?

We want some things so badly, we salivate. We sacrifice. We go into debt. We overreach. In the process, we give up more important things to have things far less important. We rob time from our kids to pursue something we haven't thought deeply about. Yet, if we get it, like Franklin's whistle, we find it's not what we thought it was cracked up to be. Peggy Lee's ballad "Is That All There Is?" comes to mind. We can't be too careful choosing what whistles we'll chase.

Arthur was often a quiet man, but a quiet one who asked good questions as I wandered about treacherous areas of life, areas filled with snares and delusions.

Unquestionably, some goals are worth pursuing, and some successes are worth having. Some will always shine. But, whether we get the big ones or not, there are plenty of little, nameless, unremembered things, like doing the wash or earning a paycheck, that, we'll see, one day, in light of eternity, as far more important than ever we imagined. But Arthur knew some of us will miss those little joys entirely.

"So be careful, Jim. More likely, regret, and not joy, will attend most of our looking back."

One year in the late 1980s, I ate several lunches in New York with a sixty-eight-year-old man who felt he was washed up. I'll call him Sam. For a year or so, only because of Arthur's example to me, I'd been trying to encourage him. Like me, Sam had come close to the edge of losing his marriage because of arrogance and blindness to his wife's needs. In his own new life of faith, Sam was learning, just as I was, how to live differently, day by day.

More than a decade has now passed since those lunches, but I still hear this melancholy man's voice sharing his regret that, as he got older, he remembered too many relationships of long ago in which he'd hurt someone. But it was too late to apologize. Time had run out; no longer could Sam make things right. That troubled him greatly and made a lasting impression on me.

"Time," Arthur once told me, "has a relentless 'one-wayness' to it; and often, we have too much of it on our hands until we don't have enough. Remember, Jim, time is not your friend. Be careful with it."

It's still the hard questions we wrestle with that shape us into mature human beings. Those hard questions come only when life sends us a bill, as it did in my marriage, and as it did again in the market's collapse during the fall of '87.

And it was Arthur who taught me to love the hard questions, or at least tolerate them, not run, or hide, from them. He asked me the deep questions of life.

So, what did he ask me? Or, as he would put it, what did he "suggest" I think about, if I wanted to grow wiser and more resilient to the bills life inevitably sends?

I'll mention just three.

First, he asked, "What is your heart set on?"

What did I *really* want, in other words. Not how much money, or where I wanted to take my next vacation, or what kind of pretty home I wanted to build one day. Or even which college I wanted my boys to go to.

He hoped I'd get those things. But whether I did or not, he wanted to know what was, above all else, most important to me. Really.

Arthur warned me to be very careful before answering this question, because few of us think deeply enough about what we want. Besides, many aren't truthful in sharing what their hearts are set on. He said we must also realize that, for good or bad, whatever we set our hearts on is, most likely, what we will get—or what we'll become. So, like Ben Franklin and his little tin whistle, Arthur urged me to be very careful what I wished for.

Dostoyevsky said it well: "Ideas have consequences."

A second question Arthur wanted me to think about was, "What do you most deeply trust?"

When I met Arthur, I trusted no one. And since I didn't know anything, or anyone, more important than me, I trusted in me. And my money. And in my ability to build networks.

Others trust in their careers. Or their brains. Or their possessions.

Or maybe their families, which may go all the way back to the *Mayflower,* which can be very important but in which I didn't place any trust.

"All of these," Arthur realized, "are worth part of your trust."

Remembering Arthur's question today, I realize that, back then, I was more likely to reflect on my choices if asked a question rather than given a lecture. So, when he asked me, "If you're really honest, Jim, what do you trust in?" I wanted to say—to please this good friend—"in God." But Arthur knew me too well. He knew I was cut from cloth that desired to please those I wanted to impress. If I'd said "in God," he would have smiled back at me and only asked his question again, because he knew I wasn't being honest.

And had I said, at that time, "I trust in God, Arthur," would that have squared with the way I spent my time? Or how I treated people, especially if I thought they were useless to me? Or with what my checkbook said?

Arthur knew it could be treacherous figuring out what we really trust. His lawyerly experience proved we all too often hide our true motivations; that is, if we even know them. We'd rather have others see us in control and mature. He thought many who can't hack real life hide out in perpetual fun-seeking, or sports. "It's just relaxation," they say. "Yes, sometimes it is," Arthur told me. "But often, it's our escape from difficulty, which, if we're over twenty, we won't readily admit."

There are lots of other ways to avoid what we need to face. He mentioned people he knew who get lost in technology. "Far beyond its power to make us more productive or, as some think, save humanity, it has tremendous power to distract or entertain us."

I learned from Arthur that for those of us who find some success in life—whatever success means to us—it can become difficult to trust in anything other than whatever that success is.

But when life's bill comes, it will demand more of us, if we live long enough. It certainly did with our family.

And we are not alone in the great challenges life has dealt us. There are many who have been tested and suffered far worse than we. A vast subgroup of people are struggling with loss and illness, unemployment and disaster, none of which is their fault. Some of these people are rich; some poor. Some are well-educated; some can barely read. But all of them have been devastated by forces beyond their control.

But I'm certain too that whatever we trust in, in time will be tested. And some who think that their business or their looks or their money are unshakable may, surprisingly, lose their faith. Life will embitter some, and jealousy will stunt others who lose what others keep taking for granted. Life is difficult and dangerous, and we need to bank our lives on what will withstand the blows that will come, sooner or later. Bad things will happen in this fallen world. Often, too, without warning.

"So, when, not if, life sends you a bill," Arthur wanted to know, "what will you do, Jim? In what will you trust? You may find yourself shocked so seriously that you will no longer know what you trust in. For if you are shocked enough, then, and only then, will you know what you really trust in."

However crisis may one day come to you, when it does come, my hope for you, as Arthur's was for me, is that whatever—or whomever—you trust will prove big enough and real enough to carry the weight of your broken dreams.

Finally, Arthur asked me, "What are you most afraid of?"

Arthur wanted to know, "What wakes you up in the middle of the night, Jim, in a cold sweat?"

"Is it looking foolish?" Arthur asked me. "Or being asked something you don't know? Maybe not fitting in? Appearing uncool or different? Losing your job? Running out of money? The death of a loved one?"

Arthur knew I, like everyone else, was afraid of something. We all are, if we're honest. But he hoped, too, that whatever I was afraid of was something important enough to be worth my fear.

Business success, as well as privileges that accompany it, can often insulate us from the dangers that lurk in the real world. We protect what we love or dread losing. And when our privileges are threatened, that can terrify us. Given what my family's been through with Lizzie's cancer and heart transplant, most of my old business fears now seem laughable. Things like losing a deal, or being overweight, or not having as large an office as someone else. How could such things have threatened me?

But they once did.

How sad, therefore, it was to read recently of a chef in France who committed suicide after a guidebook downgraded his restaurant by a single star. How tragic, too, that the heart transplanted into a friend of ours came from a beautiful young woman who killed herself over a fraudulent credit application.

The poet Carl Sandburg wrote some thoughts worth reflecting upon that might well frame the three questions Arthur put before me years ago and which still roll around in my mind today. "Limited" was how Sandburg titled his poem, like the great trains thundering across our country during the middle of the last century. The poem describes what must have been the "high technology" of rapid transport in Sandburg's day.

> I AM *riding on a limited express,*
> *one of the crack trains of the nation.*
> *Hurtling across the prairie into blue haze and dark air*
> *go fifteen all-steel coaches holding a thousand people.*
> *(All the coaches shall be scrap and rust and all the men and*
> *women laughing in the diners and sleepers shall pass to ashes.)*
> *I ask a man in the smoker where he is going*
> *and he answers: "Omaha."*[1]

We are all going to Omaha. "Omahas" of our choosing, I hope. But, maybe not. The Omaha you're speeding toward may be a life-long dream yet to come true that should you not fulfill, life may seem a failure. Or, your Omaha may be a possession that, if you got it, would shout to friend and foe alike, "I've made it!"

If your heart is set on that fancy new car, maybe that's Omaha. Maybe you should get it. But if you do, I warn you it's probably not going to be as important as you think.

Or if Omaha is that mansion on the hill you've been shooting for, go build it, if you really must. But it, too, may fail to satisfy you in the long run.

Somewhere, somehow, I hope you someday take time to think about the Omahas you're heading toward, the important ones, the ones shaping you, the ones you are becoming. Or maybe have already become.

It may not be everything you'd hoped when you were twenty-one. But that's to be expected; it's OK too. After all, to find real joy, you don't really need to win an Olympic gold medal. Or play football for the Indianapolis Colts. Or become Miss America. For none of that stuff, impressive as it is—or seemed to be once upon a time—is, in the end, all that important.

As Arthur taught me, I might never have the home or the perfect kids or the looks or the job or the things I dreamed of so long ago, either. But that's OK too. For the overwhelming part of all that stuff we dream about, or head toward, is just fantasy anyway. It's not important stuff. At least, it's not the really important stuff that matters in the long run.

But whatever it is captivating us, good or bad, that's our "Omaha." Planned or not, seen or not, we're heading there. It's likely what we'll get. Or become. And at least for a time, it will be our home, whether we want it to be or not.

Where's your Omaha?
Choose it well.

Note

1. Carl Sandburg, "Limited," *Chicago Poems* (New York: Holt, 1916), as cited in Bartleby.com.

ARTHUR, PERRY,
THE HEATHS,
AND TAKING RISKS

A favorite lunchtime haunt of mine on nice days back in Boston was any of the colonial cemeteries right in downtown. Boston has some of the oldest intact graveyards in the new world. Several famous Americans are buried in these ancient places. Names like Adams, Revere, Hancock, and Franklin abound. But what drew me to these places were less history's heavy hitters than its common citizens, the unknowns who made me wonder, "Will I be remembered?"

Some years ago a study was done of nonagenarians, people ages ninety through ninety-nine. In particular, one question they were asked stands out: "If you could live your life over, what would you do differently?"

Do you know what the old-timers said? Three things: "I'd reflect more." "I'd risk more." And, "I'd do more that might live on after me."

In spite of the runs of good fortune I knew during my best days in business, a lot of worries and fears beset me. Fear over "what if" I don't hit my numbers this quarter. Fear over what if one of my employees does something really dumb and gets me in trouble. Fear over a stock market crash. Fear over losing my job. Fear over running out of money.

Laughable stuff, maybe. But wild thoughts like that often careened around in my head. On the surface, I looked unfazed by anything; underneath, I was a worried warrior. Deeper still, below my driving ambition for more of everything, I think there was also a cry for meaning.

Wandering in the graveyards at lunch in downtown Boston, seeing the stones of people nobody knows, I asked myself again and again, "Do I matter? Does anyone care that I'm here?"

For me, right up to meeting Arthur, "Do I matter?" was one of the great questions of my life. Once I'm gone, will anyone care that I ever lived?

Coming to faith dampened that fear, but didn't extinguish it. Maybe that's why I write books now: to try to understand myself.

One day back in the late 1980s, I met Arthur at the corner of Wall and Broad Streets in lower Manhattan in front of the world headquarters of Irving Trust. (Today, like the dead in Boston, it has passed from the earth.) It was soon after I'd come to faith too, and Arthur knew I had pitifully few friends in New York who could be described as people of faith. On that day, he wanted me to meet his friend Perry, a senior guy at Irving, who wrestled often with questions of where God might be leading him.

Perry was a charming man, who radiated confidence in his work and his place in the world. He had already completed a ministry degree in the event he should have to leave the bank. Over lunch, he told me, "As far as work goes, I'm content to stay but ready to go." Interesting, I thought: Here's a free man. He felt called to go, but without something definite to go to, he wanted to do his best for Irving.

"That's the way I see it, Jim," Perry added. "God often gives us a vision of what's ahead, but doesn't give us the means to get there . . . yet. He doesn't cut the strings to where we are right away."

"But can't that make cowards of us, Perry?" I wondered out loud.

"Maybe. But whether we want to or not, our true motivation comes out. It always will. And when it does, Irving will push me out of here. I'm just not dedicated enough anymore. I know it. Some here know it too. Like sharks, they smell blood. But I don't sense it's time to go yet."

"Sounds pretty relaxed to me, Perry. Where's your fire to get going and do what matters to you?"

Perry didn't answer right away. He looked at Arthur, then me, and then leaned forward into what he hoped, I'm sure, would be a teachable moment. "Jim, don't get me wrong. Irving matters to me. So does what I'm going to do next.

"I don't know how long you've been a person of faith, but maybe this will help you. When anyone comes to know God, they'd do well to take a shovel down to the edge of an ocean and dig sand off the beach. And when a wave comes in and fills up the hole you're digging, shovel it out again. And again.

"Do you get the point? Each of us has to learn that, at least in God's kingdom, patience is the passport. There's no hurry to make things happen, to make your own success. First, and foremost, just show up. Then do the good that lies nearest. Let God set the pace."

"Wow," I thought. I, on the other hand, was already tugging on God's sleeve, telling him to "hurry up." One day—soon, I hoped—God would make me a general and a blessing to this broken world. I was in a hurry. But Perry made me think.

Since that time, I've asked many Christians, in and out of business, what they'd really like to do with their lives, if they could do anything at all.

I doubt many of them had a friend like Arthur, who took me to a friend like Perry. Because over the years what I've heard has been different from what I heard from either of them.

You know what I've heard? Things like play basketball for the Indiana Pacers. Or start a bed and breakfast in Vermont, "somewhere far away." Or be part of a crew on an America's Cup boat. One friend hoped, one day, he might conduct the Boston Pops— "even once," he said.

When my friends told me those things, I usually smiled. I felt privileged that they shared their dreams with me. Sometimes, we laughed about the dreams. And my friends were being honest with me, I know, even if their dreams made us laugh. I love my friends too. They're good people, trying to earn honest livings, supporting families, many attending church and doing good in their communities.

Still, I question my friends' goals. Those goals aren't evil, of course. But are they fitting goals, especially for people who know God, the God whose Son died for them? Do their goals show deep thought about the preciousness and brevity of life, about the urgent claims God makes on our lives, about our selfish misuse of the gifts and talents we've been given to serve this broken world? Do these goals, as Arthur gently challenged me so long ago, show real understanding of what we've received if we know God? Wrongly or not, on some level, my heart breaks for many of my friends, the Christian ones especially because so often I sense many of God's people pursue such silly goals.

Modern life doesn't encourage us to do any differently, either, as Arthur challenged me to engage in thought about where I was headed. Most of us don't want to ask ourselves hard questions. Let alone ask others.

Things like "Why am I here?" or "Why do I do the things I don't want to do and yet don't do the things I want to?" are little Chihuahuas yapping and nipping at our ankles. It's better to keep them out of the house. Maybe at three o'clock in the morning, lying awake in bed, after we've fought with our spouse or we've found we may have cancer, then maybe these questions come up. When every mistake we've made that day becomes an insurmountable problem. But that's not often.

So, we distract ourselves with little stuff, trivial stuff that's manageable; and, often, we distract others as well, to avoid thinking. Being a

Christian doesn't change that, either. Perhaps it should, but it doesn't. A lot of us act up—and act out—because, underneath, we're struggling to find meaning: the meaning of our lives.

When I finally decided to come to Huntington, Indiana, to teach college, every fear I had ever stuffed down inside me erupted like a bad case of acne. It started at the 80 percent pay cut. I'd once thought "downward mobility" could be virtuous. But this seemed crazy! What was I doing? To my family, that is, even if I could stomach the plunge?

Ironically, during my nine years after coming to know God, but before moving to Huntington, I'd received two other offers to teach at college. Both earlier offers, as well as the one from Huntington, were answers to very specific prayers I made: "Oh, Lord," I fervently pleaded, "please use my gifts and my many misspent years for your purposes. Help me to put the gifts you've given me to their highest and best use."

I prayed that prayer for nine years. And, incredibly, three times along the way, good, tenure-track teaching positions fell into my lap, positions that others would have given an ear and a toe to have. These were, I am confident, genuine answers to my prayer. But I remained fearful. I couldn't bear to look over the cliffs of my lost earnings and lifestyle. So I let the first two offers die with insincere, but very big, thank-yous. And when the Huntington College offer came along, I whined and dragged my feet for over a year before coming. Why? Because I'm human, and I was afraid. I hated losing control. Hated taking an 80 percent pay cut. It was not just looking over a cliff; it was jumping off. And I didn't want to seem like a fool to my friends!

But sometimes don't people of faith have to be fools? Or maybe "aliens," as the apostle Peter described followers of Jesus?[1]

Before I left Boston for Huntington, I used to think that if I had been asked to quit my day job and drive into inner-city Boston, I might have said "yes" quicker than I did when asked to move to Indiana. Because even inner-city Boston is close to a "real" city, unlike Indiana, which is a place that real people only fly over (or so I thought). Then, too, if I were in inner-city Boston, I might not have to give up our lovely house and pretty lifestyle.

I was being dishonest, and I knew it. As long as I stayed in Boston, I knew I was not going to work in the inner city.

In fact, it took a visit from a special young couple in 1993 to make that very point. Back then, Lizzie and I were, improbable as it may seem given our past blunders in marriage, the Sunday school teachers to the "Young Marrieds" class at the largest evangelical church in New England. Lizzie and I! Can you imagine? (Now tell me God doesn't have a sense of humor sending the two of us to teach twenty-to-thirty-something-year-olds how to be good young marrieds.)

Well, one day, Jeff and Judy Heath wanted to speak to us privately about something important, or so they said. So we invited them over for dinner, where they told us they were thinking of going to Africa as missionaries. As their "wise elders"—their term, not ours—they wanted our opinion of the wisdom of such a move. They were thinking of going for two years, before they had children or other responsibilities that would make going much harder. Mind you, this pair of Ivy League-trained engineers made good money in Boston.

"Where would you go, and what would you do?" I asked. As a businessperson, I thought I'd help them learn how to approach making a risky decision.

"To Burkina Faso, to do work with small water projects," Jeff said.

"Where?"

"Burkina Faso. On the west coast of Africa, Jim. Used to be called Upper Volta," Judy fired back.

"Oh," I said, "there."

I wondered if they needed to go so far away.

"You know, Jeff and Judy," I said, knowing they had already done extensive volunteer service in Boston, "maybe you could take a year off and do some full-time work around here, see how that feels, and where that leads."

Jeff smiled at me, but Judy was her more visibly intense self. "We could do that, yes," she said, "but you know, Jim, there are some people who want only a little bit of meaning in their lives. That's fine for them. Then, there are other people who want lots of meaning. That's us." And then she looked into me, as Arthur used to, and said, "We want to swallow it whole."

Judy had me. What could I say—that, when I was their age, looking for meaning was about as important to me as locating a left-handed saltshaker? That when I was their age, I was looking for other women? That I dreamed of making a million dollars a year? Or, should I tell them—the "wise elder" I was—that a little Christian college in Indiana had recently contacted me and wanted to know if I might like to teach there? I, who also claimed my life needed meaning but couldn't fathom giving up my money and lifestyle?

Before listening to Jeff and Judy tell us about their plans to go to Burkina Faso, I had planned to tell that little college no. But first, as a real man of God, I was going to tell Jeff and Judy what they should do with their lives in order to find meaning.

Judy's comment on "swallowing it whole" put my selfishness in a whole new light.

Lizzie's dinner was wonderful, as was our time together, even if I felt absurd that Jeff and Judy considered me their "wise elder."

"I think you have to go to Africa," I said. "From what you've said, I think God is calling you."

"We agree, Jim. Thank you," Jeff said and smiled—ready to go but content to stay.

After that night, they did go to Africa, and they are still there, now with two children. But that night caused an earthquake in me.

True, Lizzie and I were at a point in our lives where we had much more to give up than Jeff and Judy (including three sons heading off to college, high school, and elementary school, respectively). I was terrified of change, even though I'd been praying that God would use me in the highest and best way He might. And while I didn't believe then, nor do I today, that my soul's future depended on whether I went to Indiana or not, that moment, right after Judy's comment, felt as if Jesus were sitting on a log next to me.

It felt as if Jesus and I had just finished a long walk in the woods. We were both tired. It was as if Jesus then turned to me and asked something He had wanted to know for a long time.

"Jim, what do you want? For years, I've listened to your whining and complaining about how rough the business world has become, even as I've told you I need people like you there. So, when I suggest teaching opportunities in less fancy places, you say, 'Nah.'

"Please tell me, What do you want?"

That's what I heard. And in my fear, I had nothing better to say than, "I'll tell You what I want. I want all the wealth and comfort and sophistication I have back here, and I want the meaning that teaching young people might bring me, too."

And when I told Jesus that, He just sat there next to me on the log, smiling weakly, and then reached across, patted my knee, bit His lip, and looked far away.

So what did I want? I wanted as much as I could get.

When is enough enough?

For me, leaving my high-paying world was an important, if terrifying, act of faith. It pitted me against everything I thought was real. If I lost, I'd seem like a failure. Our move to Indiana threatened my competence, my shrewdness, and would likely send my settled life into chaos. Our middle son, then fifteen and more scared than I, later would say it felt as if I'd driven the family car over Niagara Falls, with everyone inside, because God had distracted me with a pretty view. But for me, it was a necessary step of faith.

Still, to sever my wife's connections to her friends and family, to sell a beautiful house with Lizzie's lovely garden, to stir up one son's deepest insecurities, these were, in the eyes of many we knew, crazy things to do. And I was crazy to do them.

I am still in touch with many of my old friends back East. Some continue to share their frustrations with me, about their work and personal lives. I ask them, when I can, "Why don't you make a change?" They answer, "I'm too old" or "The economy is too soft." Some add, "My kids or wife can't move away." Sometimes, but not often, they tell me they're afraid. They say, "You're different, Jim. You had something to go to."

Yes, I tell them, in fact, I did. It was into the path of an oncoming train.

So many good friends who outwardly seem to have everything tell me they feel they have so little. Yet, the comforts of the known make them cowards to risk what they have. Sometimes I tell them or, maybe, remind them of my own journey—of the three job offers before I could relax my grip on my own comfortable but purposeless life. "But," again they tell me, "you had good work to go to."

All kinds of voices and temptations tease and charm us throughout life. We can't help but hear them in friends we have or books we read, songs we hear or chance encounters with strangers. It's hard to figure out which ones come from God and which ones, as Ebenezer Scrooge said, may be from "an undigested bit of beef" or "a fragment of underdone potato." It's never easy; powers of discernment take time to develop and are never developed perfectly. Still, we crave knowing what we should do with our lives—which few of us will ever know with certainty.

Author Frederick Buechner gives us a hint of what is able to be known.

> *By and large, a good rule for finding . . . the kind of work [God wants you to do] is the kind of work (a) that you need most to do and (b) the world most needs to have done. If you really get a kick out of your work, you've presumably met requirement (a), but if your work is writing TV deodorant commercials, the chances are you've missed requirement (b). On the other hand, if your work is being a doctor in a leper colony, you have probably met (b), but if most of the time you're bored and depressed by it, the chances are you haven't only bypassed (a) but probably aren't helping your patients much either. Neither the hair shirt nor the soft birth will do. The place God calls you to is the place where our deep gladness and the world's deep hunger meet.*[2]

Ah, "the place where our deep gladness and the world's deep hunger meet." What a wonderful place that is to find oneself in!

Experience tells me, however, that wherever that place is, getting there will involve risk. Maybe even danger, loss of control, or a sense of incompetence—all things no one in his or her right mind invites into their lives. Stuff like that is, if we're honest, stuff we're already too acquainted with and want to avoid more of.

But the road to finding meaning lies along just such dangerous paths. For too long, many of us have relied on playing it safe, never wanting to look foolish, always trying to appear in control. But by midlife, many of us find it's just not enough: it's just not working. By then, we may have gotten control. That is, gained neat possessions. Established our competence. The very stuff we thought, back at age twenty-one, would be enough. But somewhere along life's dark ways, the safe ways let us down.

"One only lives once," Søren Kierkegaard wrote. So "if, when death comes, the life is well spent, that is, spent so that it is related rightly to eternity, then God be praised eternally. If not, then it is irremediable—one only lives once."[3]

Life is not the dress rehearsal for something else, and time is not our friend. Too many broken hearts litter this world, and too many needs go unmet. My coming to faith back in 1985 led me to serve in ways and places I never imagined. I've been to the third world. I've slung mud and laid brick in the Appalachian hills. I've been to a Jamaican orphanage and Honduran slums. But my heart hurts most for my fellow Christians in prosperous places, such as those I left back East, where people feel insignificant in spite of all they have. How hard to seem uncool, out of touch.

But in the eyes of eternity, a homemaker or a custodian serving others in gratitude may be more important than a Jerry Garcia or a Vince Lombardi. For raising a family and making a home may, in the end, ironically, be worth far more than being a Broadway actor, a rocket scientist, or a celebrity football coach. Strange as it may be, we are involved in an enterprise that goes on forever, and the ripples of lovingly serving a glass of cold water may be farther reaching than winning a Super Bowl or even a Nobel Peace Prize.

"So when is enough enough?" you may ask. "When is enough enough to calm our fears?"

I don't know. Each of us has to struggle to answer that question for himself. But few want the struggle. And many fail to answer, first, "Enough of what?" What is it we live to have more of: Money? Control? Friends? Love?

How we handle life's stresses and our own fears, such as mine about "numbers" at work, are keys to our maturity and our faith. Maturity will allow us to cope with more stress, and not run from it, or engage in too much fantasy. This is as true in the wider world as it is at home. Can we trust God even when His hand is not obvious? Can we do what we think God is telling us right now, as best we can understand it, leaving the rest to unfold as it will?

My fear over my numbers was a fear of the future. I feared that things might not turn out as I hoped. I feared they might explode out of control, wrecking what I'd worked for.

Today I see in my students' faces the same anxiety I once felt in my business life. We all feel such fears, if we're honest. It is part of being alive, because here we are still incomplete, no matter how much we have. And to deny this is to engage in fantasy or even pretend we are sovereign God.

When my students feel anxious, they sometimes tell me that feeling fearful is contrary to the will of God. In their immaturity, they feel that if they are "in God's will," then they will always feel safe, no matter what. I tell them, "You're kidding yourself. Living in a fallen world will cause every one of us to be afraid, from time to time. Feeling fear is not wrong; it's not sinful. It's what we do with our fears, whom or what we run to, that can get us in trouble—or grant us peace."

My students stress a lot about their futures because, rightly, they want to know God's will. In fact, "God's will" is probably the greatest burden Christian college students wrestle with in their spiritual lives. And what stresses them most is the fear that, if they miss God's will, they will live a life of misery.

Too often, my students—and many of us, too—see "doing" God's will as the great stress reliever.

It may work.

But often it doesn't. Because the more we try to do good, the more our stress may grow.

Paul the apostle tells us clearly how terrifying it can be to do God's will.

> [I] have worked much harder, been in prison more frequently,
> . . . and been exposed to death again and again. Five times I
> received . . . the forty lashes minus one. Three times I was
> beaten with rods, once I was stoned, three times I was ship-
> wrecked, I spent a night and a day in the open sea, I have
> been constantly on the move. I have been in danger from
> rivers, in danger from bandits, in danger from my own

*countrymen, in danger from Gentiles; in danger in the city, in
danger in the country, in danger at sea; and in danger from
false brothers. I have labored and toiled and have gone without sleep; I have known hunger and thirst and have often gone
without food; I have been cold and naked. Besides everything
else, I face daily the pressure of my concern for all the churches.
Who is weak, and I do not feel weak?*[4]

These are the words of someone doing God's will!

But Paul is not alone in feeling fear while doing God's will.
Didn't Jesus sweat blood in the Garden of Gethsemane, pleading,
"Father, may this cup be taken from me?"—all the while knowing
that His brutal cup wasn't going anywhere? Knowing the cup wouldn't
be taken away? Or, what about John the Baptist, rotting in prison,
awaiting death, asking someone to go back to Jesus and find out
whether He was "the one to come, or should we expect someone
else?"

God's will is not always clear. We kid ourselves to think it is or
can be. Sometimes it is, yes. But often it's not. Even when it is, it is
not always easy to do. Serving God, who can be a "consuming fire,"
will not always feel good, either. Nor does it always pay off in the
short run. Get used to it: feeling fear is part of being human and is
very likely part of doing God's will.

"Trust and obey, for there's no other way" are the words of a famous old hymn. Its sentiment is as true today as it was in 1887,
when it was written. Not just for people of faith, but for any seeking

a way through the dark and dangerous paths laid before life in this fallen world. Dark and dangerous and risk-filled it is, and will remain, if we have the eyes to see and courage to face the truth. The only issue to settle is whom we will obey and what we will trust in as we make our way. For we will trust and obey in someone or something.

Whatever it is, may it be worth the wager of our lives and our souls.

Notes

1. 1 Peter 2:11.

2. Frederick Buechner, *Wishful Thinking: A Theological ABC* (San Francisco: Harper SanFrancisco, 1973), 95.

3. Søren Kierkegaard, Attack upon "Christendom" (Princeton, N.J.: Princeton Univ., 1968), 245.

4. 2 Corinthians 11: 23–29.

TEN

THIS NEW
WAY OF LIFE

Les Miserables exploded onto the Broadway stage in 1986. An instant hit, it ran until the spring of 2003. I took Nicky, our oldest son, to see the play in 1987 for his twelfth birthday. He was the little guy who struggled so deeply and so young with self-esteem and depression. And it was theater that was given to him the preceding summer, in the form of a small but engaging role as a clown in a Sunday afternoon day camp performance, that began to transform his life. Now, on his birthday, I took him alone to his first Broadway play, and we sat in the second row. Because of Arthur, I was determined to become a better father.

Les Miserables, by Victor Hugo, is a timeless story of failure and redemption. Seeing *"Les Mis"* that night on Broadway with my little Nick was a great treat for both of us. And for months after, it became fodder for my conversations with Arthur (who also saw the play separately), for I was seized by one of Hugo's great themes—

that those who have been saved are saved to serve. For me, it was a variant on Jesus' challenge that to those whom much is given, much will be expected.[1] I was, perhaps, more touched by those themes than was Arthur, because they were still such new ideas for me.

As a kid, raised in the Bronx, I grew up feeling I owed no one anything. Along the way, I may have strayed, but less than bank robbers or rapists. I often wondered what my gentle friend Arthur, who'd been raised by a Harvard lawyer and a painter, could understand about going astray. To me, he was one of those rare successful people who seemed so balanced, so centered. Do such people think about straying? After all, he'd followed in his father's footsteps to Harvard, to law, and then even went to work for his old man at his firm. I was nothing like that. I was a kid from a broken home in the Bronx with a sick mother and a chip on his shoulder as big as a Ford Pinto.

Even more, before meeting Arthur, I was like the motley hero of *Les Miserables,* Jean Valjean. Like him, I had been just as certain that the only way "to make it" in this world was "my way." Like Valjean, too, I seethed from past hurt and neglect. It may not have led me, like Valjean, to steal bread. But it led me to think I needed nothing and no one outside my self-constructed networks of money and acquaintances.

As I sat in that darkened New York theater and watched God's grace break over the sorry life of Jean Valjean for the first time, grace was breaking over me as well. Unexpectedly, my eyes welled up. I was touched. For Valjean's story only continued the softening process that had begun with meeting Arthur over a year before. And though I knew I was watching a work of fiction, Valjean's story was my story.

Jean Valjean is a convict who has just been released from hard labor. He's filthy; he's broke. He's been embittered by nineteen years of injustices and ill treatment, just as I felt embittered by my upbringing. It is dinnertime, and Valjean is looking frantically for somewhere to eat and sleep. He's already been turned out of an inn, a local prison, and a nearby field. He's getting desperate.

By chance—but probably more by a gift of grace—Valjean arrives at the home of Monsignor Bonvenu—a central figure in Valjean's transformation, and, indeed, the Arthur figure in Valjean's life. Valjean is a frightful sight to the two women who care for the monsignor and his home. The housekeeper especially is suspicious. But the monsignor insists that the ex-con stay for dinner.

Nervously, the housekeeper sets the table, but she doesn't use the guest silver. The monsignor notices the oversight and gently corrects her to set the table for their special guest. Fearful, she complies. They eat well. Then, after dinner, the priest invites Valjean to spend the night in his home.

In bed that night, Valjean is in turmoil. Good and evil wrestle in mortal combat. Perplexed by the monsignor—perhaps unable to figure out his angle—he doesn't understand. Valjean is filled with fear, anger, even greed. And he can't take it. So he gets up, grabs the silver that had been set out in his honor, and heads out into the night.

Police soon find him sleeping in a field and question him about the silver he's carrying, bearing the monsignor's monogram. They assume he's a thief and drag him back to the priest, who they expect will be both relieved and outraged. But the monsignor surprises everyone. He says Valjean is telling the truth. The silver does belong to him. It was a gift from the priest himself, who then adds—more absurdly—that in Valjean's haste, he'd forgotten the silver candlesticks he'd been given, as well.

Like Valjean, I too had received a benefactor I neither expected nor deserved. Like Valjean, I couldn't understand my benefactor's "angle." And to me, everyone had an angle. No one did the kinds of things Arthur did for me, especially, without expecting something back. And not without owning part of me afterwards. It was impossible for me, at first, to believe that all he wanted was to bless me. Like Valjean, I was, early on, no more accepting of grace than Valjean was.

In that theater that night, Valjean and his monsignor became me and my Arthur.

At last, with the police gone, Monsignor Bonvenu is alone with Valjean. He looks deep into the crook's eyes and tells him, "Jean Valjean, my brother, you belong no longer to evil, but to good. It is your soul that I am buying for you. I withdraw it from dark thoughts and from the spirit of hell, and I give it to God."

Arthur never said those words to me. I was not a convicted felon or a fall-down drunk or a heroin addict. But the monsignor's sentiments were unmistakably Arthur's.

Now, of course, Valjean is shocked; he expected punishment,

and deserved it, too. But instead the priest's act of grace begins a transformation of Valjean's life. What prison couldn't do—it only hardened him—one single, extravagant act of wildly generous human kindness brings Valjean to conversion. Just as Arthur's friendship had done to me.

The petty thief turned hardened criminal begins to become a blessing to the world. Transfixed by the drama, sitting next to my Nicky that night, how much I hoped, one day, I too might become a blessing to this broken and needy world!

Les Miserables is fiction, but fiction can be powerful. It can touch parts of us that may be too tender to touch more directly. Stories can, as this one did for me, prod us to see the immense power grace can impart, and the duty its coming brings.

If, like Valjean, at long last and miraculously, I had begun to awaken to a different sort of life, and had just begun to come to my senses, I knew now, even if only sketchily, that I had been saved from the emptiness of my old life for a purpose: to bless others. And for any of us who have also been saved from destructive lives, the truth is the same: We have been saved to serve.

We, who have been shown this new way of life, must try to live it. As Arthur told me, "We're the lucky ones." But with a gift comes a responsibility to share our good fortune with others. And, as Arthur did with me, with sensitivity and humility.

When my eventful *Tres Dias* weekend in Connecticut came to a misty close, my retreat leader hugged me and whispered in my ear, "Christ is counting on you."

At the time, I confess, I didn't have a clue what he meant. But a year and a half later, at a Broadway play, I began to understand what that leader might have been getting at. And at that moment in New York City, I vowed that, as long as I live, I would try never to say "no" to God. I vowed that, as much as it would be within my power, the change Arthur started in me would not have been for nothing.

Though I might not have the chance to change a life as dramatically as Arthur had affected me, or the fictional Monsignor Bonvenu did Valjean, we never know when angels are in our midst or needy souls are being chased by devils. Each of us probably knows of real people who have been Monsignor Bonvenus—or Arthurs—to us or someone else. That night in New York, with Nicky, I knew what I wanted out of life: I wanted to become one of those people.

To want less would be to trivialize the gift of new life that Arthur, as an ambassador of God, imparted to me.

Les Miserables was a powerful, convicting but early step in my own transformation from death to life. It was just a beginning in my understanding of the power a good friend can have to impart a scandalous blessing.

I know for myself I once was dead and was brought back to life through a friend. He introduced me to the Eternal, when I thought all I needed was a quick divorce.

I know too that if saving leads to serving, then those who have been saved from much will have the most expected of them. And quite possibly, those who have been saved will suffer, as well, as part of their service.

Arthur became an unexpected hero to me. But before I knew him, like many who grew up in the wild '60s, I fantasized about becoming a truly independent person, my own man. The type of guy who, as Frank Sinatra sang, "did it my way" and was proud of it, too.

Once upon a time—and for so long a time—central to my dreams of independence and lack of accountability was money. I believed money was my ticket to tell those around me, should they annoy me or not like something I did, "Drop dead! I'm outta here!"

When I shared that secret fantasy with Arthur, he thought I sounded like James Bond. And while I never was a Bond fan, I saw his point. Bond had the kind of smashingly self-possessed, brilliant competence that I wanted to see in myself yet knew I didn't have. The kind of self-mastery and control that, no matter what life throws at you, you won't just survive, you'll triumph and make others pay for messing with you.

Yes, once upon a time, I wanted to be one of those.

While Bond was an invention (as was Jean Valjean), I thought Arthur might be right: I did want to be like Bond. The guy had an irresistible star quality, so intriguing to competitive business types like me. Bond is the ultimate "go-to," "can-do" guy. And what's more, he lives the life to prove it, with his toys, clothes, and women. And, just as I was, in my own way, Bond is devoted to greatness; first of all, his own. He knows how to take risks, handle danger, and live high. And as I once was, he's addicted to winning, as all highly successful, competitively-driven businesspeople are. His entire personality is built around being, or becoming, invincible. For to lose would bring irreversible shame. In spite of my laughing early on, when Arthur exposed my Bondish fantasies, he may have been right. At least he made me think.

"I kid you not, Jim. Bond's in us all. In you and me too."

Arthur never argued against dedication or hard work. He never suggested, as did a particularly holy friend of mine who was in Alcoholics Anonymous, "Let go and let God." Arthur never told me not to have goals or dreams, or to go after them. If he had, I would have dismissed Arthur, because I don't think "what will be will be" would have gotten Arthur to first base with me, a boy from the Bronx who was determined "to make it."

Still, Arthur was careful to coach me not to be my own hero, like so many others I knew. He thought too many men, whether they know it or not, choose to live life unrealistically, as would-be heroes who can never fail, never need help, and never find themselves out of control.

My friendship with Arthur taught me that an idealist can be grounded in reality. I didn't expect that from a person of faith. For I once thought of idealists or people of faith as brittle—tourists, perhaps—in this rough world where I lived and competed. They might say they were "in the world but not of it." But too often, with my chip hanging off my shoulder, they seemed out of touch and, sometimes, even out of their minds.

But not Arthur. He was the first person of faith to share his Harvard accomplishments with me, as well as the sadness of his divorce. And that made all the difference. He was real. And because he was real, I trusted him.

He urged me not to minimize any gift, even strange gifts like suffering and reversal. "Wounds are redeemable too," he told me. "Whatever life inflicts on you can be useful to help others." We can, if we are willing, help others by sharing the struggles that have challenged our own lives. They can help someone else make sense of their life. They can be used at work, at home, with neighbors, to befriend, encourage, challenge, or comfort too. It's part of God's work for us— comforting others with the comfort we have received from God.

Amazing, isn't it? All the junk that happens to us throughout our lives can, through grace, become a healing balm to others, if we have the courage to share our lives wisely. Arthur showed me that too. He took a risk to share a part of his life that was not perfect, that seemed, frankly, like utter failure. He did so with gentleness, at the right moments. And it changed my life.

"God wastes nothing," Arthur told me. "Our saddest moments and deepest failures can become redemptive for ourselves and for others." Yet, too often, even people of faith may feel they must hide their sorrows and present the watching world only the phony veneer of an effortless perfection.

What a lost opportunity, as I learned from Arthur's own example. If any of us has known God's comfort in our own troubles (and who hasn't?), who better might be able to help than we who have shared life's struggles? And, maybe, along the way, through our concern, we can say a kind word on behalf of God.

Gilda Radner, the funny woman from *Saturday Night Live* back in the 1980s, made millions laugh as "Roseanne Roseannadanna." She said funny things, like: "Did you ever stub your big toe on the car or drop something heavy on your foot and the toenail on the big toe turns different colors like purple and brown and green and then it hangs there and falls off in your sock? And you're left with a toe with no nail and a sock that has a nail in it."[2]

Gilda was one funny lady, for whom many of us are thankful. But few may know of an even greater gift she gave us, having nothing to do with being funny.

Radner died in 1989, after a two-and-a-half-year battle with ovarian cancer. Though I used to think she was the funniest woman in the world, now I also think she's among the bravest, and the wisest too. She's a hero of mine. Like Arthur. Like Lizzie.

In her autobiography, *It's Always Something*, which didn't appear until after her death, she wrote,

> *I wanted to be able to write on the book jacket: "Her triumph over cancer" or "She wins the cancer war." I wanted a perfect ending, so I sat down to write the book with the ending in place before there even was an ending. Now I've learned, the hard way, that some poems don't rhyme and some stories don't have a clear beginning, middle and end. Like my life, this book has ambiguity. Like my life, this book is about not knowing, having to change, taking the moment and making the best of it, without knowing what's going to happen next. Delicious ambiguity.*[3]

None of us knows about tomorrow. People like Gilda and my Lizzie, and the bad breaks they got in life, teach us a lot. But they teach us especially, when you come right down to it, life is really just the gift of time. And how much time any of us gets is not known to any of us here while we're in the midst of whatever time we get. So if there's something you've always wanted to do, I'd suggest that, if it's worth doing, do it. Now.

Once upon a time, I thought that I had the world in the palm of my hand. Yet, I was miserable. I didn't know the value of what I had, yet I thought, whatever was over the next hill or after the next deal would bring real fulfillment. Things would be different, and things would keep getting better. Or so I hoped.

Then I met Arthur, and my life really began to change. But this didn't happen quickly, totally, easily, or without risk. But change I did, and I still think the change was for the better.

That weekend I went away to the retreat Arthur wooed me to, the weekend that began to change my life big time, I was given a little prayer card that I still carry. It says much about what I had just begun to learn from Arthur, and I'll be learning until the day I die.

O God, for another day, for another morning,
for another hour, for another minute, for another chance
to live and serve Thee, I am truly grateful.
Do Thou this day free me
from all fear of the future,
from all anxiety about tomorrow,

from all bitterness towards any one,
from all cowardice in the face of danger,
from all laziness in the face of work,
from all failure before opportunity,
from all weakness when Thy power is at hand.
But fill me
with Love that knows no barrier,
with Sympathy that reaches to all,
with Courage that cannot be shaken,
with Faith strong enough for the darkness,
with Strength sufficient for my task,
with Wisdom to meet life's complexities,
with Power to lift me to Thee.
Be Thou with me for another day, and use me as Thou wilt.
For Christ's sake, I pray. Amen.[4]

God be with you.

Notes

1. See Luke 12:48.

2. As quoted on the Internet at http://www.angelfire.com/ny3/gildaradner/Quotes.html.

3. Gilda Radner, *It's Always Something* (New York: Simon & Schuster, 1989), 268.

4. "My Morning Prayer," used by permission of the Open Church Foundation, PO Box 81389, Wellesley Hills, MA 02481-0004.

In 1994 the mayor of Mount Vernon, New York, gave my friend Arthur the key to his city for Arthur's years of service in the city's food kitchen. That same year, Arthur and his wife, Ariane, moved to Colorado to continue their retirement years.

Though now a thousand miles apart, Arthur and I have kept in touch, mostly by phone and e-mail. However, at Thanksgiving 1996, the first Thanksgiving after my Lizzie received her heart transplant, our family flew to Colorado to be with him and Ariane. What more fitting way to spend so significant a milestone in our lives? Then in May of 2001, as Arthur was approaching open-heart surgery, I visited him in a Denver intensive care unit, and, again, got the chance to stay at his home, but this time only with Ariane and one of Arthur's sons.

As this book was being written, I asked Arthur to read over the manuscript. With great humility, even embarrassment, he agreed. I asked him to reflect on the nature and impact of our relationship that began more than twenty years ago. In his words are clues to how any person can be, or might become, an "Arthur," a person who encourages, mentors, and in the process, unconsciously lives and passes along a genuine, humble faith. In Arthur's words, I also hear echoes of why every one of us needs a good friend.

I was astounded upon first reading the manuscript of *Walking with Arthur.*

Yes, my name is Arthur. Yes, Jim O'Donnell is a dear friend. Yes, he and I have shared much with each other. But frankly, I do not recognize the Arthur depicted in those early chapters. In no way do I mean that Jim is distorting his experience. Rather his characterization of the person he calls Arthur is simply far from the image I have of myself.

To me, the substance of what Jim recalls sounds more like the work of the Holy Spirit, introducing a prism into Jim's perceptions of me and what I did. Jim saw and heard only what he needed to in order to bring him closer to God.

I find it wonderful that I may have been used in such a way, but I never set out to make Jim my "project" on behalf of God. Our times together bring to mind a sentence in the devotional writings of Oswald Chambers: "The lives that have been the greatest blessing to you are the lives of those people who themselves were unaware of having been a blessing."[1]

The real story here is that the author and I met, and we became friends—trusting friends. Simple as that. I happened to bring into that friendship my own relatively new relationship with God. I had a slight head start over Jim on this walk of faith not because I am twenty years his senior but because I had been truly changed a few months earlier by my own *Tres Dias* weekend.[2] And since I had been so affected, I wondered if Jim would like to attend a similar weekend.

Curiously, my own experience with *Tres Dias* had first been suggested to me by my wife, Ariane. You see, we really do just pass along our faith from one to the other. But to do that, we have to risk getting close to someone else.

Having been spiritually awakened on my own weekend, I learned a simple new truth: that one does not come to know and grow in God alone. I had discovered that one of the elements of a truly joyful Christian life is finding a trusting friend, or—if we are really blessed—a couple of friends with whom we can, and do, share our joys and sorrows, our strengths and weaknesses.

Such friends become those to whom we can look for help, correction, encouragement, and support in overcoming the mistakes and shortcomings every one of us will encounter, if we are honest, along our way.

A friend, such as Jim, though it's not clear from the book, challenged me to confront my own mistakes and shortcomings. This beautiful process of mutual help and support only works when there is mutual openness and integrity. It only happens when we put down our defenses and let our friends see us as we are.

Such friends, and small groups of friends, are rare, unfortunately. My quest for such a group, after my own spiritual renewal began, met with many frustrations. I looked at, and called, a number of churches and pastors in my area with no success. But when, at last, I contacted the pastor of the Pelham church, where I was not a member, he responded, "I need a small group too." At last, I thought, somebody understood.

That small step led to the gathering, in December of 1984, of that group of men mentioned in chapter 3. To that group, first, I brought and then found a brilliant, inquiring, and searching mind in Jim O'Donnell. He became my friend, a friend I could truly trust. He also had a mind that could help me understand the Bible as we read it together. I never had the feeling I was leading him. Rather, I felt I was learning from him.

We were on this walk together. We shared a friendship, every bit as nourishing to my faith as it evidently proved to his.

We were learning from each other.

All too frequently in fearing we might display weakness, we profess to others that we have the answers. In truth, however, we don't even know the questions. How much better it has been to be open and honest, to admit our ignorance, to work together on gaining understanding, on growing in our faith. In those open exchanges, we can see our true selves, which is the first step in growing spiritually.

In reading *Walking with Arthur,* I sense the Holy Spirit has only committed one of His usual, yet often unnoticed, miracles in bringing Jim O'Donnell and Arthur together. The Spirit colored our perceptions of one another as the motivating force in the relationship, only to spur on our mutual growth and maturity.

I am astonished and fortunate to have been so used. But the truth is that if I had been given Jim's teaching and writing skills, I would be writing a book called *Walking with Jim.*

Notes

1. Oswald Chambers, *My Utmost For His Highest,* devotional for August 31, Chambers, special updated ed., James Reimann, ed. (n.p.: Oswald Chambers Publication Association), 1995.

2. *Tres Dias,* Spanish for "three days," is the three-day weekend Jim and I experienced—an ecumenical, lay-led, offspring of *Cursillo De Christandad* ("a short course in Christian Living"). The *Cursillo* has its roots in the Spanish Catholic church, with the first *Cursillo* weekend held in Majorca in 1949. The program was brought to the United States by Spanish fliers training in Texas, and the first *Tres Dias* in America was held in Newburgh, New York, in 1972. Today *Tres Dias* communities thrive in many states and foreign countries, all lay-led and ecumenical.

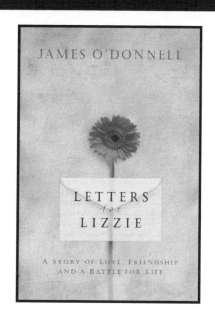

A Story of Love, Friendship and a Battle for Life

"A mature and gritty account of wrestling with God and what it means to be a 'new creation.'"

—Publishers Weekly Religion Bookline

"Not just for those people facing a serious challenge but for anyone who needs real encouragement and a renewal of perspective."

—Gary J. Oliver, The Center for Marriage and Family Studies, John Brown University

Letters for Lizzie   ISBN: 1-881273-01-6
by James O'Donnell   EAN/ISBN-13: 978-1-881273-01-1

WALKING WITH ARTHUR TEAM

ACQUIRING EDITOR
Mark Tobey

BACK COVER COPY
Lisa Ann Cockrel

COPY EDITOR
Jim Vincent

COVER DESIGN
Paetzold Associates

INTERIOR DESIGN
Ragont Design

PRINTING AND BINDING
Versa Press, Inc.

The typeface for the text of this book is
AGaramond